ETHICAL AND RELIGIOUS CLASSICS OF EAST AND WEST

Volume 7

GOD AND MAN

GOD AND MAN
In the Old Testament

LEON ROTH

Taylor & Francis Group
LONDON AND NEW YORK

First published in Great Britain in 1955 by George Allen & Unwin Ltd.

This edition first published in 2022
by Routledge
2 Park Square, Milton Park, Abingdon, Oxon OX14 4RN

and by Routledge
605 Third Avenue, New York, NY 10158

Routledge is an imprint of the Taylor & Francis Group, an informa business

© 1955 George Allen & Unwin Ltd

All rights reserved. No part of this book may be reprinted or reproduced or utilised in any form or by any electronic, mechanical, or other means, now known or hereafter invented, including photocopying and recording, or in any information storage or retrieval system, without permission in writing from the publishers.

Trademark notice: Product or corporate names may be trademarks or registered trademarks, and are used only for identification and explanation without intent to infringe.

British Library Cataloguing in Publication Data
A catalogue record for this book is available from the British Library

ISBN: 978-1-03-213267-9 (Set)
ISBN: 978-1-00-324156-0 (Set) (ebk)
ISBN: 978-1-03-214794-9 (Volume 7) (hbk)
ISBN: 978-1-03-214799-4 (Volume 7) (pbk)
ISBN: 978-1-00-324113-3 (Volume 7) (ebk)

DOI: 10.4324/9781003241133

Publisher's Note
The publisher has gone to great lengths to ensure the quality of this reprint but points out that some imperfections in the original copies may be apparent.

Disclaimer
The publisher has made every effort to trace copyright holders and would welcome correspondence from those they have been unable to trace.

GOD AND MAN
IN THE OLD TESTAMENT

by

LEON ROTH
D.Phil., F.B.A.

LONDON: GEORGE ALLEN & UNWIN LTD
NEW YORK: THE MACMILLAN COMPANY

FIRST PUBLISHED IN 1955

This book is copyright under the Berne Convention. Apart from any fair dealing for the purposes of private study, research, criticism or review, as permitted under the Copyright Act 1911, no portion may be reproduced by any process without written permission. Enquiry should be made to the publisher.

© *George Allen & Unwin Ltd.*

PRINTED IN GREAT BRITAIN
BY C. TINLING AND CO. LTD
LIVERPOOL, LONDON AND PRESCOT

To the memory of
J. L. MAGNES

'*For Zion's sake will I not hold my peace*'

In some five hundred passages ranging in length from half verses to whole chapters, this Biblical anthology attempts to bring together, in their original wording, the highest expressions of the Biblical view of life with its hopes, its promises, its obligations and, together with them, its sanctions and its warnings.

The anthology follows a plan and method of its own. It is non-historical and non-doctrinal and rests on the conviction that great literature is adequate to all times and all occasions. It starts with the confrontations of man with God as seen in the 'calls' of the prophets, and proceeds to the ways of life demanded of man and the duties accompanying the privilege of vocation. It ends with the visions of the ideal society which in times of trial like the present have always served to sustain the mind.

GENERAL INTRODUCTION

AS A RESULT of two Wars that have devastated the World men and women everywhere feel a twofold need. We need a deeper understanding and appreciation of other peoples and their civilizations, especially their moral and spiritual achievements. And we need a wider vision of the Universe, a clearer insight into the fundamentals of ethics and religion. How ought men to behave? How ought nations? Does God exist? What is His Nature? How is He related to His creation? Especially, how can man approach Him? In other words, there is a general desire to know what the greatest minds, whether of East or West, have thought and said about the Truth of God and of the beings who (as most of them hold) have sprung from Him, live by Him, and return to Him.

It is the object of this Series, which originated among a group of Oxford men and their friends, to place the chief ethical and religious masterpieces of the world, both Christian and non-Christian, within easy reach of the intelligent reader who is not necessarily an expert—the ex-Service man who is interested in the East, the undergraduate, the adult student, the intelligent public generally. The Series will contain books of three kinds: translations, reproductions of ideal and religious art, and background books showing the surroundings in which the literature and art arose and developed. These books overlap each other. Religious art, both in East and West, often illustrates a religious text, and in suitable cases the text and the pictures will be printed together to complete each other. The background books will often consist largely of translations. The volumes will be prepared by scholars of distinction, who will try to make them, not only scholarly, but intelligible and enjoyable. This Introduction represents the views of the General Editors as to the scope of the Series, but not necessarily the views of all contributors to it. The contents of the books will also be very varied—ethical and social, biographical, devotional, philosophic and mystical, whether in poetry, in pictures or in prose. There is a great wealth of material. Confucius lived in a time much like our own, when State was at war with State and the people suffering and disillusioned; and the 'Classics' he preserved or inspired show the social virtues that may unite families, classes and States into one great family, in obedience to the Will of Heaven. Asoka and Akbar (both of them great patrons of art) ruled a vast Empire on the principles of religious faith. There are the moral anecdotes and moral maxims of the Jewish and Muslim writers of the Middle Ages. There are the beautiful tales of courage, love and fidelity in the Indian and Persian epics. Shakespeare's plays show that he thought the true relation between man and man is love. Here and there a volume will illustrate the unethical or less ethical man and difficulties that beset him.

Then there are the devotional and philosophic works. The lives and legends (legends often express religious truth with clarity and beauty) of the Buddha, of the parents of Mary, of Francis of Assisi, and the exquisite sculptures and paintings that illustrate them. Indian and Christian religious music, and the words of prayer and praise which the music intensifies. There are the prophets and apocalyptic writers, Zarathustrian and Hebrew; the Greek philosophers, Christian thinkers— and the Greek, Latin, medieval and modern—whom they so deeply influenced. There is, too, the Hindu, Buddhist and Christian teaching expressed in such great monuments as the Indian temples, Barabudur (the Chartres of Asia) and Ajanta, Chartres itself and the Sistine Chapel.

Finally, there are the mystics of feeling, and the mystical philosophers. In God-loving India the poets, musicians, sculptors and painters inspired by the spiritual worship of Krishna and Rama, as well as the philosophic mystics from the Upanishads onward. The two great Taoists Lao-tze and Chuang-tze and the Sung mystical painters in China, Rumi and other sufis in Islam, Plato and Plotinus, followed by 'Dionysius', Eckhart, St. John of the Cross and (in our view) Dante and other great mystics and mystical painters in many Christian lands.

Mankind is hungry, but the feast is there, though it is locked up and hidden away. It is the aim of this Series to put it within reach, so that, like the heroes of Homer, we may stretch forth our hands to the good cheer laid before us.

No doubt the great religions differ in fundamental respects. But they are not nearly so far from one another as they seem. We think they are further off than they are largely because we so often misunderstand and misrepresent them. Those whose own religion is dogmatic have often been as ready to learn from other teachings as those who are liberals in religion. Above all, there is an enormous amount of common ground in the great religions, concerning, too, the most fundamental matters. There is frequent agreement on the Divine Nature; God is the One, Self-subsisting Reality, knowing Himself, and therefore loving and rejoicing in Himself. Nature and finite spirits are in some way subordinate kinds of Being, or merely appearances of the Divine, the One. The three stages of the way of man's approach or return to God are in essence the same in Christian and non-Christian teaching: an ethical stage, then one of knowledge and love, leading to the mystical union of the soul with God. Each stage will be illustrated in these volumes.

Something of all this may (it is hoped) be learnt from the books and pictures in this Series. Read and pondered with a desire to learn, they will help men and women to find 'fulness of life', and peoples to live together in greater understanding and harmony. To-day the earth is beautiful, but men are disillusioned and afraid. But there may come a day, perhaps not a distant day, when there will be a renaissance of man's spirit: when men will be innocent and happy amid the beauty of the world, or their eyes will be opened to see that egoism and strife are folly, that the universe is fundamentally spiritual, and that men are the sons of God.

> They shall not hurt nor destroy
> In all My holy mountain:
> For all the earth shall be full of the
>   knowledge of the Lord
> As the waters cover the sea.
>   THE EDITORS

FOREWORD

This anthology was prompted by the twofold belief that the Hebrew Scriptures have something of importance to communicate and that they can communicate it best themselves. The selection given is not exhaustive. The topics are restricted and within each topic the treatment is far from complete. But it is offered in the hope that it may be suggestive and even, on occasion, helpful. Its material is old, some of it possibly the oldest literature in which mankind has shown continuous interest. But its relevance is renewed with the years. It is what students have learned to call mature. At its best it has achieved a serenity and a penetration which set it both inside and above all situations.

Scholars will gasp at my gay disregard of philological and historical considerations; and I confess to have stitched my cloth as it pleased me, taking sentences, even phrases, from any context that occurred and setting them beside others similarly displaced. This is due not only to ignorance. Literature produces its effect in many ways; and it is just the isolated sentence or detached phrase which sticks in the mind and is called out long after by an appropriate occasion. Ideas germinate unseen; and their first origin is often an unheeded word embedded in the memory fortuitously.

But my motley is a context of its own; and I should ask readers, in the words of Robert Bridges in the Introduction to his Spirit of Man, *to 'bathe rather than to fish in these waters'. But I shall quote, if I may, a few whole sentences from this Introduction to the best of all anthologies known to me, in order to explain my own method and approach:*

'First then, the reader is invited to bathe rather than to fish in these waters: that is to say, the several pieces are to *be read in context; and it is for this reason that no titles nor names of authors are inserted in the text, because they would distract the attention and lead away the thought and even overrule consideration. Yet, although there is a sequence of context, there is no logical argument: the demonstration is of various moods of mind, which are allowed free play. . . . As for the sequence chosen, that might no doubt have been other than it is without damage and perhaps with advantage; but, as will readily be perceived, the main implication is essential, namely, . . .'*

—but what the implication is in this case I leave to the reader who will, I hope, judge for himself.

*

In the interests of space I have occasionally omitted a few verses from a passage but never in such a way as to alter the sense; and I have always noted the omission in the reference. As a rule, and except when otherwise indicated, I have used the Revised Version of 1884 (text or margin). In the few cases where I have felt compelled to modify it I have indicated the fact by adding an A (=*Amended*) *in brackets after the reference.* (M) *after a reference means* (R.V.) *Margin. I should perhaps say that I have found the principal defect of the Revised Version, apart from its lack of divination of future scholarship, its frequent and disturbing changes of the word order of the original. Where I have changed it back I have indicated the fact by the addition to the reference of the letters* OA (=*Order Amended*). *But I am afraid that in any case, as was remarked over two thousand years ago, 'things originally spoken in Hebrew have not the same force in them when they are translated into another tongue'.*

*

Much modern religion seems to be of the type so happily

described by M. Robert de Traz in his study of *Pierre Loti* (*Hachette, 1948, p. 133*):

'... Sa préoccupation religieuse se fait lancinante. Elle lui dicte de nouveaux voyages qui sont moins des explorations de pays inconnus que des pèlerinages à la découverte du divin. C'est maintenant une aventure spirituelle qu'il poursuit.

'Elle n'aboutira pas; elle ne fera même qu'aggraver sa tristesse, sa déception, son scepticisme. Pourquoi?

'C'est que cette quête de la divinité est encore et toujours, chez Loti, une recherche complaisante de lui-même. Il agréera ... ce qui correspond à ses propres préférences; il n'acceptera pas les exigences ... Il ambitionne moins d'atteindre à la vérité que de calmer son angoisse latente, sa terreur de la fin qui s'approche, et de trouver enfin moins une certitude peut-être qu'un remède et une consolation.'

It is by contrast with such an attitude as this, so widespread in our time, that the nature of Biblical religion stands out.

Cambridge,   L. R.
   11 March 1954.

CONTENTS

	Page
GENERAL INTRODUCTION	9
FOREWORD	13
I *The Vision of the Almighty*	19
II *The Knowledge of the Most High*	29
III *The Everlasting God*	36
IV *Our Days on the Earth*	47
V *The God of the Spirits of All Flesh*	55
VI *In Thee I Trust*	67
VII *The Path of Life*	78
VIII *The Ten Words*	91
IX *Everyone According to his Ways*	121
X *My People, My Chosen*	130
XI *The God of Judgement*	141
XII *A Remnant Shall Return*	150
XIII *The Vision for the Appointed Time*	161
XIV *The End of the Matter*	168

ONE

THE VISION OF THE ALMIGHTY[1]

*The voice of the Lord crieth unto the city,
and the man of wisdom will see thy name.*[2]

It has become fashionable to talk of the relationship between God and man as that of a dialogue. That is as may be; but it should at least be noted that the dialogue involved is not a tea-table conversation. It is rather a call, even a calling to account; and it is curious to observe from the record how some of those called upon found in it terror and suffering and how some, for varying reasons, tried to evade it.

After some preliminary skirmishing I offer their plain tales, together with some embellishments and general reflections.

And the Lord God called unto the man, and said unto him, Where art thou?[3]

And the Lord God said unto the woman, What is this thou hast done?[4]

And the Lord said unto Cain, Where is Abel thy brother? And he said, I know not: am I my brother's keeper?
And he said, What hast thou done?[5]

And when the sun was going down, a deep sleep fell upon Abram; and, lo, an horror of great darkness fell upon him.[6]

[1] Num. 24: 4.
[2] Mic. 6: 9.
[3] Gen. 3: 9.
[4] Gen. 3: 13.
[5] Gen. 4: 9–10.
[6] Gen. 15: 12.

And Jacob awaked out of his sleep, and he said, Surely the Lord is in this place; and I knew it not. And he was afraid, and said, How awesome is this place![1]

And he said, Hear now my words: if there be a prophet among you, I the Lord will make myself known unto him in a vision, I will speak with him in a dream. My servant Moses is not so; he is faithful in all mine house: with him will I speak mouth to mouth, even manifestly, and not in dark speeches.[2]

Now Moses was keeping the flock of Jethro his father in law, the priest of Midian: and he led the flock to the back of the wilderness, and came to the mountain of God, unto Horeb. And the angel of the Lord appeared unto him in a flame of fire out of the midst of a bush: and he looked, and, behold, the bush burned with fire, and the bush was not consumed. And Moses said, I will turn aside now, and see this great sight, why the bush is not burnt.

And when the Lord saw that he turned aside to see, God called unto him out of the midst of the bush, and said, Moses, Moses. And he said, Here am I.

And he said, Draw not nigh hither.[3]

And Moses said unto the Lord, Oh Lord, I am not eloquent, neither heretofore, nor since thou hast spoken unto thy servant: for I am slow of speech, and of a slow tongue.

And the Lord said unto him, Who hath made man's mouth? or who maketh a man dumb, or deaf, or seeing, or blind? is it not I the Lord? Now therefore go, and I will be with thy mouth, and teach thee what thou shalt speak.

[1]Gen. 28: 16–17(A). [2]Num. 12: 6–8. [3]Exod. 3: 1–5.

And he said, Oh Lord, send, I pray thee, by the hand of him whom thou wilt send.[1]

And it came to pass on the third day, when it was morning, that there were thunders and lightnings, and a thick cloud upon the mount, and the voice of a trumpet exceeding loud; and all the people that were in the camp trembled.

And Moses brought forth the people out of the camp to meet God; and they stood at the nether part of the mount.[2]

God came from Teman,
And the Holy One from mount Paran. [Selah
His glory covered the heavens,
And the earth was full of his praise.
And his brightness was as the light;
He had rays coming forth from his hand:
And there was the hiding of his power.
  Before him went the pestilence,
And fiery bolts went forth at his feet.
He stood, and measured the earth;
He beheld, and drove asunder the nations:
And the eternal mountains were scattered,
The everlasting hills did bow.[3]

And ye came near and stood under the mountain; and the mountain burned with fire unto the heart of heaven, with darkness, cloud, and thick darkness. And the Lord spake unto you out of the midst of the fire: ye heard the voice of words, but ye saw no form; only ye heard a voice.[4]

[1]Exod. 4: 10–13.   [2]Exod. 19: 16–17.   [3]Hab. 3: 3–6.   [4]Deut. 4: 11–12.

Hearken ye unto the noise of his voice,
And the sound that goeth out of his mouth.
He sendeth it forth under the whole heaven,
And his lighting unto the ends of the earth.
After it a voice roareth;
He thundereth with the voice of his majesty:
And he stayeth them not when his voice is heard.
  God thundereth marvellously with his voice;
Great things doeth he, which we cannot comprehend.[1]

And the child Samuel ministered unto the Lord before Eli. And the word of the Lord was precious in those days; there was no open vision.

And it came to pass at that time, when Eli was laid down in his place, (now his eyes had begun to wax dim, that he could not see,) and the lamp of God was not yet gone out, and Samuel was laid down to sleep, in the temple of the Lord, where the ark of God was; that the Lord called Samuel: and he said, Here am I. And he ran unto Eli, and said, Here am I; for thou calledst me. And he said, I called not; lie down again. And he went and lay down.

And the Lord called yet again, Samuel. And Samuel arose and went to Eli, and said, Here am I; for thou calledst me. And he answered, I called not, my son; lie down again. Now Samuel did not yet know the Lord, neither was the word of the Lord yet revealed unto him.

And the Lord called Samuel again the third time. And he arose and went to Eli, and said, Here am I; for thou calledst me. And Eli perceived that the Lord had called the child. Therefore Eli said unto Samuel, Go, lie down: and it shall be, if he call thee, that thou

[1] Job 37: 2–5.

shalt say, Speak, Lord; for thy servant heareth. So Samuel went and lay down in his place.

And the Lord came, and stood, and called as at other times, Samuel, Samuel. Then Samuel said, Speak; for thy servant heareth.[1]

And, behold, the word of the Lord came to him, and he said unto him, What doest thou here, Elijah? And he said, I have been very jealous for the Lord, the God of hosts; for the children of Israel have forsaken thy covenant, thrown down thine altars, and slain thy prophets with the sword: and I, even I only, am left; and they seek my life, to take it away.

And he said, Go forth, and stand upon the mount before the Lord.

And, behold, the Lord passed by, and a great and strong wind rent the mountains, and brake in pieces the rocks before the Lord; but the Lord was not in the wind: and after the wind an earthquake; but the Lord was not in the earthquake: and after the earthquake a fire; but the Lord was not in the fire: and after the fire a still small voice.

And it was so, when Elijah heard it, that he wrapped his face in his mantle, and went out, and stood in the entering in of the cave. And, behold, there came a voice unto him, and said, What doest thou here, Elijah?[2]

In the year that king Uzziah died I saw the Lord sitting upon a throne, high and lifted up, and his train filled the temple. Above him stood the seraphim: each one had six wings; with twain he covered his face, and with twain he covered his feet, and with twain he did

---

[1] 1 Sam. 3: 1-10.   [2] 1 Kings 19: 9-13.

fly. And one cried unto another, and said, Holy, holy, holy, is the Lord of hosts: the whole earth is full of his glory.

And the foundations of the thresholds were moved at the voice of him that cried, and the house was filled with smoke. Then said I, Woe is me! for I am undone; because I am a man of unclean lips, and I dwell in the midst of a people of unclean lips: for mine eyes have seen the King, the Lord of hosts.

Then flew one of the seraphim unto me, having a live coal in his hand, which he had taken with the tongs from off the altar: and he touched my mouth with it, and said, Lo, this hath touched thy lips; and thine iniquity is taken away, and thy sin purged.

And I heard the voice of the Lord, saying, Whom shall I send, and who will go for us? Then I said, Here am I; send me.

And he said, Go.[1]

Now the word of the Lord came unto me, saying, Before I formed thee in the belly I knew thee, and before thou camest forth out of the womb I sanctified thee; I have appointed thee a prophet unto the nations.

Then said I, Ah, Lord God! behold, I cannot speak: for I am a child. But the Lord said unto me, Say not, I am a child: for to whomsoever I shall send thee thou shalt go, and whatsoever I shall command thee thou shalt speak. Be not afraid because of them: for I am with thee to deliver thee, saith the Lord.

Then the Lord put forth his hand, and touched my mouth; and the Lord said unto me, Behold, I have put my words in thy mouth.[2]

[1]Isa. 6: 1–9. [2]Jer. 1: 4–9.

O Lord, thou hast deceived me, and I was deceived: thou art stronger than I, and hast prevailed; I am become a laughingstock all the day, every one mocketh me. For as often as I speak, I cry out; I cry, Violence and spoil: because the word of the Lord is made a reproach unto me, and a derision, all the day.

And if I say, I will not make mention of him, nor speak any more in his name, then there is in mine heart as it were a burning fire shut up in my bones, and I am weary with forbearing, and I cannot contain.[1]

Is not my word like as fire? saith the Lord; and like a hammer that breaketh the rock in pieces?[2]

Now it came to pass in the thirtieth year, in the fourth month, in the fifth day of the month, as I was among the captives by the river Chebar, that the heavens were opened, and I saw visions of God.

In the fifth day of the month, which was the fifth year of king Jehoiachin's captivity, the word of the Lord came expressly unto Ezekiel the priest, the son of Buzi, in the land of the Chaldeans by the river Chebar; and the hand of the Lord was there upon him.

And I looked, and, behold, a stormy wind came out of the north, a great cloud, with a fire infolding itself, and a brightness round about it, and out of the midst thereof as the colour of amber, out of the midst of the fire. And out of the midst thereof came the likeness of four living creatures. . . . And over the head of the living creature there was the likeness of a firmament, like the colour of the terrible crystal, stretched forth over their heads above. And under the firmament were their wings straight, the one toward the other: every one had two which covered on this side, and every one

[1]Jer. 20: 7-9.   [2]Jer. 23: 29.

had two which covered on that side, their bodies. And when they went, I heard the noise of their wings like the noise of great waters, like the voice of the Almighty, a noise of tumult like the noise of an host: when they stood, they let down their wings.

And there was a voice above the firmament that was over their heads: when they stood, they let down their wings. And above the firmament that was over their heads was the likeness of a throne, as the appearance of a sapphire stone: and upon the likeness of the throne was a likeness as the appearance of a man upon it above. And I saw as the colour of amber, as the appearance of fire within it round about, from the appearance of his loins and upward; and from the appearance of his loins and downward I saw as it were the appearance of fire, and there was brightness round about him. As the appearance of the bow that is in the cloud in the day of rain, so was the appearance of the brightness round about. This was the appearance of the likeness of the glory of the Lord. And when I saw it, I fell upon my face, and I heard a voice of one that spake.

And he said unto me, Son of man, stand upon thy feet, and I will speak with thee.[1]

Also the word of the Lord came unto me, saying, Son of man, behold, I take away from thee the desire of thine eyes with a stroke: yet neither shalt thou mourn nor weep, neither shall thy tears run down. Sigh, but not aloud; make no mourning for the dead, bind thy headtire upon thee, and put thy shoes upon thy feet, and cover not thy lips, and eat not the bread of men.

So I spake unto the people in the morning; and at even my wife died.[2]

[1] Ezek 1: 1-5; 22-2:1.   [2] Ezek. 24: 15-18.

I heard, and my belly trembled,
My lips quivered at the voice;
Rottenness entered into my bones, and I trembled in
 my place.[1]

I lifted up mine eyes, and looked, and behold a man clothed in linen, whose loins were girded with pure gold of Uphaz: his body also was like the beryl, and his face as the appearance of lightning, and his eyes as lamps of fire, and his arms and his feet like in colour to burnished brass, and the voice of his words like the voice of a multitude.

And I Daniel alone saw the vision: for the men that were with me saw not the vision; but a great quaking fell upon them, and they fled to hide themselves. So I was left alone, and saw this great vision, and there remained no strength in me: for my comeliness was turned in me into corruption, and I retained no strength. Yet heard I the voice of his words; and when I heard the voice of his words, then was I fallen into a deep sleep on my face, with my face toward the ground.

And, behold, a hand touched me, which set me upon my knees and upon the palms of my hands. And he said unto me, O Daniel, thou man greatly beloved, understand the words that I speak unto thee, and stand upright; for unto thee am I now sent: and when he had spoken this word unto me, I stood trembling.[2]

Fear came upon me, and trembling,
Which made all my bones to shake.
Then a spirit passed before my face;
The hair of my flesh stood up.
It stood still, but I could not discern the appearance
 thereof;

[1]Hab. 3: 16.   [2]Dan. 10: 5-11.

A form was before mine eyes;
There was silence, and I heard a voice.[1]

I am no prophet, neither am I a prophet's son; but I am an herdman, and a dresser of sycomore trees: and the Lord took me from following the flock, and the Lord said unto me, Go, prophesy unto my people Israel.[2]

The Lord God hath given me the tongue of them that are taught, that I should know how to sustain with words him that is weary: he wakeneth morning by morning, he wakeneth mine ear to hear as they that are taught.[3]

The lion hath roared, who will not fear? the Lord God hath spoken, who can but prophesy?[4]

[1]Job 4: 14–16. [2]Amos 7: 14–15 (m). [3]Isa. 50: 4. [4]Amos 3: 8.

TWO

THE KNOWLEDGE OF THE MOST HIGH[1]

Who is the Lord, that I should hearken unto his voice?[2]

The God of the Hebrew Scriptures does not reveal himself simply (Section 1). He reveals himself as of a certain character. It is a commonplace that this character is what we are accustomed to call moral. But some of the expressions of this fact and its implications are of startling freshness. I do not refer so much to the stories of, e.g., Abraham teaching the higher morality to God or God handing on the lesson to Jonah, as to such serene affirmations as those with which the present Section opens and concludes.

Thus saith the Lord, The heaven is my throne, and the earth is my footstool: what manner of house will ye build unto me? and what place shall be my rest?

For all these things hath mine hand made, and so all these things came to be, saith the Lord: but to this man will I look, even to him that is poor and of a contrite spirit, and that trembleth at my word.[3]

But will God in very deed dwell on the earth? behold, heaven and the heaven of heavens cannot contain thee; how much less this house that I have builded![4]

For thus saith the high and lofty One that inhabiteth eternity, whose name is Holy: I dwell in the high and

[1]Num. 24: 16.   [2]Exod. 5: 2.   [3]Isa. 66: 1–2.   [4]1 Kings 8: 27.

holy place, with him also that is of a contrite and humble spirit, to revive the spirit of the humble, and to revive the heart of the contrite ones.[1]

Righteousness and judgement are the foundation of
    thy throne:
Mercy and truth go before thy face.[2]

And Abraham drew near, and said, Wilt thou consume the righteous with the wicked? Peradventure there be fifty righteous within the city: wilt thou consume and not spare the place for the fifty righteous that are therein? That be far from thee to do after this manner, to slay the righteous with the wicked, that so the righteous should be as the wicked; that be far from thee: shall not the Judge of all the earth do right?

And the Lord said, If I find in Sodom fifty righteous within the city, then I will spare all the place for their sake.

And Abraham answered and said, Behold now, I have taken upon me to speak unto the Lord, which am but dust and ashes: peradventure there shall lack five of the fifty righteous: wilt thou destroy all the city for lack of five? And he said, I will not destroy it, if I find there forty and five.

And he spake unto him yet again, and said, Peradventure there shall be forty found there. And he said, I will not do it for the forty's sake.

And he said, Oh let not the Lord be angry, and I will speak: peradventure there shall thirty be found there. And he said, I will not do it, if I find thirty there.

And he said, Behold now, I have taken upon me to speak unto the Lord: peradventure there shall be

[1] Isa. 57: 15.   [2] Ps. 89: 14.

twenty found there. And he said, I will not destroy it for the twenty's sake.

And he said, Oh let not the Lord be angry, and I will speak yet but this once: peradventure ten shall be found there. And he said, I will not destroy it for the ten's sake.[1]

Run ye to and fro through the streets of Jerusalem, and see now, and know, and seek in the broad places thereof, if ye can find a man, if there be any that doeth justly, that seeketh truth; and I will pardon her.[2]

Being full of compassion he forgiveth iniquity and
    destroyeth not:
Yea, many a time turneth he his anger away,
And doth not stir up all his wrath.[3]

I will not execute the fierceness of mine anger, I will not return to destroy Ephraim: for I am God, and not man.[4]

Full of compassion and gracious, slow to anger, and plenteous in mercy and truth.[5]

A father of the fatherless, and a judge of the widows, Is God in his holy habitation.[6]

The Lord, the habitation of justice.[7]

In thee the fatherless findeth mercy.[8]

For the Lord your God, he is God of gods, and Lord of lords, the great God, the mighty, and the terrible, which regardeth not persons, nor taketh reward. He

[1] Gen. 18: 23–32. [3] Ps. 78: 38 (A). [5] Exod. 34: 6. [7] Jer. 50: 7.
[2] Jer. 5: 1. [4] Hos. 11: 9. [6] Ps. 68: 5. [8] Hos. 14: 4.

doth execute the judgement of the fatherless and widow, and loveth the stranger, in giving him food and raiment.[1]

Ye shall not afflict any widow, or fatherless child. If thou afflict them in any wise, and they cry at all unto me, I will surely hear their cry.[2]

If thou at all take thy neighbour's garment to pledge, thou shalt restore it unto him by that the sun goeth down: for that is his only covering, it is his garment for his skin: wherein shall he sleep? and it shall come to pass, when he crieth unto me, that I will hear; for I am gracious.[3]

The Lord is slow to anger, and great in power, and will by no means clear the guilty: the Lord hath his way in the whirlwind and in the storm, and the clouds are the dust of his feet. He rebuketh the sea, and maketh it dry, and drieth up all the rivers: Bashan languisheth, and Carmel, and the flower of Lebanon languisheth. The mountains quake at him, and the hills melt; and the earth is upheaved at his presence, yea, the world, and all that dwell therein.

Who can stand before his indignation? and who can abide in the fierceness of his anger? his fury is poured out like fire, and the rocks are broken asunder by him.

The Lord is good, a strong hold in the day of trouble; and he knoweth them that put their trust in him.[4]

The Lord is good to all;
And his tender mercies are over all his works.[5]

And the word of the Lord came unto Jonah the second time, saying, Arise, go unto Nineveh, that great city,

[1]Deut. 10: 17–18. [2]Exod. 22: 26–27. [3]Ps. 145: 9.
[2]Exod. 22: 22–23. [4]Nahum 1: 3–7.

and preach unto it the preaching that I bid thee. So Jonah arose, and went unto Nineveh, according to the word of the Lord. Now Nineveh was an exceeding great city, of three days' journey. And Jonah began to enter into the city a day's journey, and he cried, and said, Yet forty days, and Nineveh shall be overthrown. And the people of Nineveh believed God; and they proclaimed a fast, and put on sackcloth, from the greatest of them even to the least of them.

And the tidings reached the king of Nineveh, and he arose from his throne, and laid his robe from him, and covered him with sackcloth, and sat in ashes. And he made proclamation and published through Nineveh by the decree of the king and his nobles, saying, Let neither man nor beast, herd nor flock, taste any thing: let them not feed, nor drink water: but let them be covered with sackcloth, both man and beast, and let them cry mightily unto God: yea, let them turn every one from his evil way, and from the violence that is in their hands. Who knoweth whether God will not turn and repent, and turn away from his fierce anger, that we perish not?

And God saw their works, that they turned from their evil way; and God repented of the evil, which he said he would do unto them; and he did it not.

But it displeased Jonah exceedingly, and he was angry. And he prayed unto the Lord, and said, I pray thee, O Lord, was not this my saying, when I was yet in my country? Therefore I hasted to flee unto Tarshish: for I knew that thou art a gracious God, and full of compassion, slow to anger, and plenteous in mercy, and repentest thee of the evil. Therefore now, O Lord, take I beseech thee, my life from me; for it is better for me to die than to live.

And the Lord said, Doest thou well to be angry?

Then Jonah went out of the city, and sat on the east side of the city, and there made him a booth, and sat under it in the shadow, till he might see what would become of the city. And the Lord God prepared a gourd, and made it to come up over Jonah, that it might be a shadow over his head, to deliver him from his evil case. So Jonah was exceeding glad because of the gourd. But God prepared a worm when the morning rose the next day, and it smote the gourd, that it withered. And it came to pass, when the sun arose, that God prepared a sultry east wind; and the sun beat upon the head of Jonah, that he fainted, and requested for himself that he might die, and said, It is better for me to die than to live.

And God said to Jonah, Doest thou well to be angry for the gourd? And he said, I do well to be angry even unto death.

And the Lord said, Thou hast had pity on the gourd, for the which thou hast not laboured, neither madest it grow; which came up in a night, and perished in a night: and should not I have pity on Nineveh, that great city; wherein are more than sixscore thousand persons that cannot discern between their right hand and their left hand; and also much cattle?[1]

Thy faithfulness reacheth unto the skies.
Thy righteousness is like the mountains of God;
Thy judgements are a great deep:
O Lord, thou preservest man and beast.[2]

The Lord upholdeth all that fall,
And raiseth up all those that be bowed down.
The eyes of all wait upon thee;
And thou givest them their meat in due season.

[1] Jonah 3–4. [2] Ps. 36: 5–6.

Thou openest thine hand,
And satisfiest the desire of every living thing.
The Lord is righteous in all his ways,
And gracious in all his works.
The Lord is nigh unto all them that call upon him,
To all that call upon him in truth.[1]

Seek ye the Lord while he may be found, call ye upon him while he is near: let the wicked forsake his way, and the unrighteous man his thoughts: and let him return unto the Lord, and he will have mercy upon him ; and to our God, for he will abundantly pardon.[2]

He delighteth in mercy.[3]

Thus saith the Lord, Let not the wise man glory in his wisdom, neither let the mighty man glory in his might, let not the rich man glory in his riches: but let him that glorieth glory in this, that he understandeth, and knoweth me, that I am the Lord which exercise loving-kindness, judgement, and righteousness, in the earth: for in these things I delight, saith the Lord.[4]

For I desire mercy, and not sacrifice; and the knowledge of God more than burnt offerings.[5]

He judged the cause of the poor and needy; then it was well. Was not this to know me? saith the Lord.[6]

[1]Ps. 145: 14–18.
[2]Isa. 55: 6–7.
[3]Mic. 7: 18.
[4]Jer. 9: 23–24.
[5]Hos. 6: 6.
[6]Jer. 22: 16.

THREE

THE EVERLASTING GOD[1]

I am the Lord, that maketh all things.[2]

Some religious thinkers try to defend the moral character of God by slurring over his responsibility as everlasting and omnipresent creator. The burden of the Biblical account would seem to be that it is just the everlasting and omnipresent creator who is, and should be expected to be, responsible. The questions of Job remain questions; but they are swallowed up by the counter-questionings of God.

And God said unto Moses, I AM THAT I AM.[3]

And even to old age I am he, and even to hoar hairs will I carry you: I have made, and I will bear; yea, I will carry, and will deliver.[4]

Of old hast thou laid the foundation of the earth;
And the heavens are the work of thy hands.
They shall perish, but thou shalt endure:
Yea, all of them shall wax old like a garment;
As a vesture shalt thou change them, and they shall
    be changed:
But thou art the same,
And thy years shall have no end.[5]

I am the first, I also am the last. Yea, mine hand hath laid the foundation of the earth, and my right hand hath spread out the heavens.[6]

[1] Isa. 40: 28. [3] Exod. 3: 14. [5] Ps. 102: 25–27.
[2] Isa. 44: 24. [4] Isa. 46: 4. [6] Isa. 48: 12–13.

By the word of the Lord were the heavens made;
And all the host of them by the breath of his mouth.[1]

The heavens are thine, the earth also is thine:
The world and the fulness thereof, thou hast founded them.[2]

Thou makest the outgoings of the morning and
    evening to rejoice.
  Thou visitest the earth, and waterest it,
Thou greatly enrichest it;
The river of God is full of water:
Thou providest them corn, when thou hast so prepared the earth.
Thou waterest her furrows abundantly;
Thou settest the ridges thereof:
Thou makest it soft with showers;
Thou blessest the springing thereof.
Thou crownest the year with thy goodness;
And thy paths drop fatness.
They drop upon the pastures of the wilderness:
And the hills are girded with joy.
  The pastures are clothed with flocks;
The valleys also are covered over with corn;
They shout for joy, they also sing.[3]

The day is thine, the night also is thine:
Thou hast prepared the light and the sun.
Thou hast set all the borders of the earth:
Summer and winter, thou hast made them.[4]

While the earth remaineth, seedtime and harvest, and cold and heat, and summer and winter, and day and night shall not cease.[5]

[1] Ps. 33: 6.
[2] Ps. 89: 11.
[3] Ps. 65: 8–13.
[4] Ps. 89: 16–17 (OA).
[5] Gen. 8: 22.

Yea, the stork in the heaven knoweth her appointed times; and the turtle and the swallow and the crane observe the time of their coming.[1]

For he spake, and it was done;
He commanded, and it stood fast.[2]

Which have placed the sand for the bound of the sea, by a perpetual decree, that it cannot pass it; and though the waves thereof toss themselves, yet can they not prevail; though they roar, yet can they not pass over it.[3]

He stretcheth out the north over empty space,
And hangeth the earth upon nothing.[4]

He is wise in heart, and mighty in strength:
Who hath hardened himself against him, and prospered?
  Which removeth the mountains, and they know it not,
When he overturneth them in his anger.
Which shaketh the earth out of her place,
And the pillars thereof tremble.
Which commandeth the sun, and it riseth not;
And sealeth up the stars.
Which alone stretcheth out the heavens,
And treadeth upon the waves of the sea.
Which maketh the Bear, Orion, and the Pleiades,
And the chambers of the south.
  Which doeth great things past finding out;
Yea, marvellous things without number.[5]

In the beginning God created the heaven and the earth. And the earth was waste and void; and darkness

[1] Jer. 8: 7.
[2] Ps. 33: 9.
[3] Jer. 5: 22.
[4] Job 26: 7.
[5] Job 9: 4-10.

was upon the face of the deep: and the spirit of God moved upon the face of the waters. And God said, Let there be light: and there was light.[1]

Bless the Lord, O my soul.
   O Lord my God, thou art very great;
Thou art clothed with honour and majesty.
Who coverest thyself with light as with a garment;
Who stretchest out the heavens like a curtain:
Who layeth the beams of his chambers in the waters;
Who maketh the clouds his chariot;
Who walketh upon the wings of the wind:
Who maketh winds his messengers;
His ministers a flaming fire:
Who laid the foundations of the earth,
That it should not be moved for ever.
   Thou coveredst it with the deep as with a vesture;
The waters stood above the mountains.
At thy rebuke they fled;
At the voice of thy thunder they hasted away;
They went up by the mountains, they went down by
    the valleys,
Unto the place which thou hadst founded for them.
Thou hast set a bound that they may not pass over;
That they turn not again to cover the earth.
   He sendeth forth springs into the valleys;
They run among the mountains:
They give drink to every beast of the field;
The wild asses quench their thirst.
By them the fowl of the heaven have their habitation,
They sing among the branches.
He watereth the mountains from his chambers:
The earth is satisfied with the fruit of thy works.

[1] Gen. 1: 1.

> He causeth the grass to grow for the cattle,
> And herb for the service of man;
> That he may bring forth food out of the earth:
> And wine that maketh glad the heart of man,
> And oil to make his face to shine,
> And bread that strengtheneth man's heart.
> The trees of the Lord are satisfied;
> The cedars of Lebanon, which he hath planted;
> Where the birds make their nests;
> As for the stork, the fir trees are her house.
> The high mountains are for the wild goats ;
> The rocks are a refuge for the conies.
> He appointed the moon for seasons:
> The sun knoweth his going down.
> Thou makest darkness, and it is night;
> Wherein all the beasts of the forest do creep forth.
> The young lions roar after their prey,
> And seek their meat from God.
> The sun ariseth, they get them away,
> And lay them down in their dens.
> Man goeth forth to his work
> And to his labour until the evening.
> O Lord, how manifold are thy works!
> In wisdom hast thou made them all:
> The earth is full of thy riches.
> Yonder is the sea, great and wide,
> Wherein are things creeping innumerable,
> Both small and great beasts.
> There go the ships;
> There is leviathan, whom thou hast formed to take his
>   pastime therein.
> These wait all upon thee,
> That thou mayest give them their meat in due season.
> That thou givest unto them they gather;
> Thou openest thy hand, they are satisfied with good.

Thou hidest they face, they are troubled;
Thou takest away their breath, they die,
And return to their dust.
Thou sendest forth thy spirit, they are created;
And thou renewest the face of the ground.
   Let the glory of the Lord endure for ever;
Let the Lord rejoice in his works:
Who looketh on the earth, and it trembleth;
He toucheth the mountains, and they smoke.
   I will sing unto the Lord as long as I live:
I will sing my praise to my God while I have any being.
Let my meditation be sweet unto him:
I will rejoice in the Lord.
Let sinners be consumed out of the earth,
And let the wicked be no more.
   Bless the Lord, O my soul.[1]

And God saw everything that he had made, and, behold, it was very good.[2]

Praise the Lord from the earth,
Ye sea-monsters, and all deeps:
Fire and hail, snow and vapour;
Stormy wind, fulfilling his word:
Mountains and all hills;
Fruitful trees and all cedars:
Beasts and all cattle;
Creeping things and flying fowl:
   Kings of the earth and all peoples;
Princes and all judges of the earth:
Both young men and maidens;
Old men and children:
Let them praise the name of the Lord.[3]

[1] Ps. 104.   [2] Gen. 1: 31.   [3] Ps. 148: 7–13 (M).

He hath made the earth by his power, he hath established the world by his wisdom.[1]

But where shall wisdom be found?
And where is the place of understanding?[2]

The Lord formed me as the beginning of his way,
The first of his works of old.
I was set up from everlasting, from the beginning,
Or ever the earth was.
When there were no depths, I was brought forth;
When there were no fountains abounding with water.
Before the mountains were settled,
Before the hills was I brought forth;
While as yet he had not made the earth, nor the fields,
Nor the beginning of the dust of the world.
When he established the heavens, I was there:
When he set a circle upon the face of the deep:
When he made firm the skies above:
When the fountains of the deep became strong:
When he gave to the sea its bound,
That the waters should not transgress his commandment:
When he marked out the foundations of the earth:
 Then I was by him, as a master workman:
And I was daily his delight,
Rejoicing always before him;
Rejoicing in his habitable earth;
And my delight was with the sons of men.[3]

Surely I am more brutish than any man,
And have not the understanding of a man:
And I have not learned wisdom,
Neither have I the knowledge of the Holy One.

[1]Jer. 10: 12.   [2]Job 28: 12.   [3]Prov. 8: 22-31 (M).

Who hath ascended up into heaven, and descended?
Who hath gathered the wind in his fists?
Who hath bound the waters in his garment?
Who hath established all the ends of the earth?
What is his name, and what is his son's name, if
    thou knowest?[1]

Who is this that darkeneth counsel
By words without knowledge?
Gird up now thy loins like a man;
For I will demand of thee, and declare thou unto me.
    Where wast thou when I laid the foundations of the
        earth?
Declare, if thou hast understanding.
Who determined the measures thereof, if thou knowest?
Or who stretched the line upon it?
Whereupon were the foundations thereof fastened?
Or who laid the corner stone thereof;
When the morning stars sang together,
And all the sons of God shouted for joy?
    Or who shut up the sea with doors,
When it brake forth, as if it had issued out of the womb?
When I made the cloud the garment thereof,
And thick darkness a swaddlingband for it,
And prescribed for it my decree,
And set bars and doors,
And said, Hitherto shalt thou come, but no further;
And here shall thy proud waves be stayed?
    Hast thou commanded the morning since thy days
        began,
And caused the dayspring to know its place;
That it might take hold of the ends of the earth,
And the wicked be shaken out of it?

[1] Prov. 30: 2-4.

It is changed as clay under the seal;
And all things stand forth as a garment:
And from the wicked their light is withholden,
And the high arm is broken.
   Hast thou entered into the springs of the sea?
Or hast thou walked in the recesses of the deep?
Have the gates of death been revealed unto thee?
Or hast thou seen the gates of the shadow of death?
Hast thou comprehended the breadth of the earth?
Declare, if thou knowest it all.
   Where is the way to the dwelling of light,
And as for darkness, where is the place thereof;
That thou shouldest take it to the bound thereof,
And that thou shouldst discern the paths to the house
    thereof?
Doubtless, thou knowest, for thou wast then born,
And the number of thy days is great!
   Hast thou entered the treasuries of the snow,
Or hast thou seen the treasuries of the hail,
Which I have reserved against the time of trouble,
Against the day of battle and war?
By what way is the light parted,
Or the east wind scattered upon the earth?
Who hath cleft a channel for the waterflood,
Or a way for the lightning of the thunder;
To cause it to rain on a land where no man is;
On the wilderness, wherein there is no man;
To satisfy the waste and desolate ground;
And to cause the tender grass to spring forth?
   Hath the rain a father?
Or who hath begotten the drops of dew?
Out of whose womb came the ice?
And the hoary frost of heaven, who hath gendered it?
The waters are hidden as with stone,
And the face of the deep is frozen.

Canst thou bind the cluster of the Pleiades,
Or loose the bands of Orion?
Canst thou lead forth the Mazzaroth in their season?
Or canst thou guide the Bear with her train?
Knowest thou the ordinances of the heavens?
Canst thou establish the dominion thereof in the earth?
Canst thou lift up thy voice to the clouds,
That abundance of waters may cover thee?
Canst thou send forth lightnings, that they may go,
And say unto thee, Here we are?
    Who hath put wisdom in the inward parts?
Or who hath given understanding to the mind?
Who can number the clouds by wisdom?
Or who can pour out the bottles of heaven,
When the dust runneth into a mass,
And the clods cleave fast together?
    Wilt thou hunt the prey for the lioness?
Or satisfy the appetite of the young lions,
When they couch in their dens,
And abide in the covert to lie in wait?
    Who provideth for the raven his food,
When his young ones cry unto God,
And wander for lack of meat?[1]

He giveth to the beast his food,
And to the young ravens which cry.[2]

I am the Lord, and there is none else. I form the light, and create darkness; I make peace, and create evil; I am the Lord, that doeth all these things.[3]

Except the Lord build the house,
They labour in vain that build it:
Except the Lord keep the city,
The watchman waketh but in vain.[4]

[1] Job 38.   [2] Ps. 147: 9.   [3] Isa. 45: 6–7.   [4] Ps. 127: 1.

Hast thou not known? hast thou not heard? the everlasting God, the Lord, the Creator of the ends of the earth, fainteth not, neither is weary; there is no searching of his understanding. He giveth power to the faint; and to him that hath no might he increaseth strength.[1]

Which made heaven and earth,
The sea, and all that in them is;
Which keepeth truth for ever;
Which executeth judgement for the oppressed;
Which giveth food to the hungry:
The Lord looseth the prisoners;
The Lord openeth the eyes of the blind;
The Lord raiseth up them that are bowed down;
The Lord loveth the righteous;
The Lord preserveth the strangers;
He upholdeth the fatherless and widow.[2]

Know ye that the Lord he is God:
It is he that hath made us, and we are his.[3]

Forsake not the works of thine own hands.[4]

---

[1] Isa. 40: 28–29. [2] Ps. 146: 6–9. [3] Ps. 100: 3. [4] Ps. 138: 8.

FOUR

OUR DAYS ON THE EARTH[1]

Ye are strangers and sojourners with Me.[2]

All ancient peoples were pre-Victorian, and the Bible shares with Homer an untainted vision of the miseries of the human state. Yet if it is the part of wisdom to make this recognition a basis of our view of life, it is not, as the next Section will show, the sole basis; and the very existence of the spirit of revolt suggests that there is something to revolt for and even someone to appeal to.

For we needs must die, and are as water spilt on the ground, which cannot be gathered up again.[3]

I shall go to him, but he shall not return to me.[4]

Few and evil have been the days of the years of my life.[5]

For we are strangers before thee, and sojourners, as all our fathers were: our days on the earth are as a shadow, and there is no abiding.[6]

And he remembered that they were but flesh;
A wind that passeth away, and cometh not again.[7]

Man that is born of woman
Is of few days, and full of trouble.

[1] 1 Chron. 29: 13.   [2] 2 Sam. 14:14.   [4] Gen. 47: 9.   [7] Ps. 78: 39.
[3] Lev. 25: 23.   [3] 2 Sam. 12: 23.   [6] 1 Chron. 29: 15.

He cometh forth like a flower, and is cut down:
He fleeth also as a shadow, and continueth not.[1]

Is there not a warfare to man upon earth?
And are not his days like the days of an hireling?
As a servant that earnestly desireth the shadow,
And as an hireling that looketh for his wages:
So am I made to possess months of vanity,
And wearisome nights are appointed to me.
When I lie down, I say,
When shall I arise? but the night is long;
And I am full of tossings to and fro unto the dawning
 of the day.
 My flesh is clothed with worms and clods of dust;
My skin closeth up and breaketh out afresh.
My days are swifter than a weaver's shuttle,
And are spent without hope.
Oh remember that my life is wind:
Mine eye shall no more see good.
The eye of him that seeth me shall behold me no more:
Thine eyes shall be upon me, but I shall not be.
As the cloud is consumed and vanisheth away,
So he that goeth down to Sheol shall come up no more.
He shall return no more to his house,
Neither shall his place know him any more.
 Therefore I will not refrain my mouth;
I will speak in the anguish of my spirit;
I will complain in the bitterness of my soul.
Am I a sea, or a sea-monster,
That thou settest a watch over me?
When I say, My bed shall comfort me,
My couch shall ease my complaint;
Then thou scarest me with dreams,
And terrifiest me through visions:

[1] Job 14: 1-2.

So that my soul chooseth strangling,
And death rather than these my bones.
   I loathe my life; I would not live alway;
Let me alone; for my days are vanity.
What is man, that thou shouldest magnify him,
And that thou shouldest set thine heart upon him,
And that thou shouldest visit him every morning,
And try him every moment?
How long wilt thou not look away from me,
Nor let me alone till I swallow down my spittle?
   If I have sinned, what do I unto thee, O thou watcher of men?
Why hast thou set me as a mark for thee,
So that I am a burden to myself?
And why dost thou not pardon my transgressions and take away mine iniquity?
For now shall I lie down in the dust;
And thou shalt seek me diligently, but I shall not be.[1]

For the living know that they shall die: but the dead know not any thing, neither have they any more a reward; for the memory of them is forgotten. As well their love, as their hatred and their envy, is now perished; neither have they any more a portion for ever in any thing that is done under the sun.[2]

Lord, make me to know mine end,
And the measure of my days, what it is;
Let me know how frail I am.
Behold, thou hast made my days as handbreadths;
And mine age is as nothing before thee:
Surely every man at his best estate is altogether vanity.
   Surely every man walketh in a vain shew: [Selah

[1] Job 7.   [2] Eccles. 9: 5–6.

Surely they are disquieted in vain:
He heapeth up riches, and knoweth not who shall gather them.
And now, Lord, what wait I for?
My hope is in thee.
Deliver me from all my transgressions:
Make me not the reproach of the foolish.
I was dumb, I opened not my mouth;
Because thou didst it.
Remove thy stroke away from me:
I am consumed by the blow of thine hand.
When thou with rebukes dost correct man for iniquity,
Thou makest his beauty to consume away like a moth:
Surely every man is vanity. [Selah
Hear my prayer, O Lord, and give ear unto my cry;
Hold not thy peace at my tears:
For I am a stranger with thee,
A sojourner, as all my fathers were.
O spare me, that I may recover strength,
Before I go hence, and be no more.[1]

Rejoice, O young man, in thy youth: and let thy heart cheer thee in the days of thy youth, and walk in the ways of thine heart, and in the sight of thine eyes: but know thou, that for all these things God will bring thee into judgement. Therefore remove sorrow from thy heart, and put away evil from thy flesh: for youth and the prime of life are vanity.

Remember also thy Creator in the days of thy youth, or ever the evil days come, and the years draw nigh, when thou shalt say, I have no pleasure in them; or ever the sun, and the light, and the moon, and the stars, be darkened, and the clouds return after the

---

[1] Ps. 39: 5-14.

rain: in the day when the keepers of the house shall tremble, and the strong men shall bow themselves, and the grinders cease because they are few, and those that look out of the windows be darkened, and the doors shall be shut in the street; when the sound of the grinding is low, and one shall rise up at the voice of a bird, and all the daughters of music shall be brought low; yea, they shall be afraid of that which is high, and terrors shall be in the way; and the almond tree shall blossom, and the grasshopper shall be a burden, and the caper-berry shall fail: because man goeth to his long home, and the mourners go about the streets:

Or ever the silver cord be loosed, or the golden bowl be broken, or the pitcher be broken at the fountain, or the wheel broken at the cistern; and the dust return to the earth as it was, and the spirit return unto God who gave it.

Vanity of vanities, saith the Preacher; all is vanity.[1]

As for man, his days are as grass;
As a flower of the field, so he flourisheth.
For the wind passeth over it, and it is gone;
And the place thereof shall know it no more.
   But the mercy of the Lord is from everlasting to everlasting upon them that fear him,
And his righteousness unto children's children.[2]

The voice of one saying, Cry. And one said, What shall I cry? All flesh is grass, and all the goodliness thereof is as the flower of the field:

The grass withereth, the flower fadeth; because the breath of the Lord bloweth upon it; surely the people is grass. The grass withereth, the flower fadeth: but the word of our God shall stand for ever.[3]

[1]Eccles. 11: 9–12: 8.   [2]Ps. 103: 15–17.   [3]Isa. 40: 6–8.

But God will redeem my soul from the power of Sheol:
For he shall receive me. [Selah
  Be thou not afraid when one is made rich,
When the glory of his house is increased:
For when he dieth he shall carry nothing away;
His glory shall not descend after him.
Though while he lived he blessed his soul,
And men praise thee, when thou doest well to thyself,
He shall go to the generation of his fathers;
They shall never see the light.
  Man that is in honour, and understandeth not,
Is like the beasts that perish.[1]

O Lord, thou hast searched me, and known me.
Thou knowest my downsitting and mine uprising,
Thou understandest my thought afar off.
Thou searchest out my path and my lying down,
And art acquainted with all my ways.
For there is not a word in my tongue,
But, lo, O Lord, thou knowest it altogether.
Thou hast beset me behind and before,
And laid thine hand upon me.
Such knowledge is too wonderful for me;
It is high, I cannot attain unto it.
  Whither shall I go from thy spirit?
Or whither shall I flee from thy presence?
If I ascend up into heaven, thou art there:
If I make my bed in Sheol, behold, thou art there.
If I take the wings of the morning,
And dwell in the uttermost parts of the sea;
Even there shall thy hand lead me,
And thy right hand shall hold me.
If I say, Surely the darkness shall overwhelm me,
And the light about me shall be night;

[1] Ps. 49: 15–20.

Even the darkness hideth not from thee,
But the night shineth as the day:
The darkness and the light are both alike to thee.
   For thou hast possessed my reins:
Thou hast covered me in my mother's womb.
I will give thanks unto thee; for I am fearfully and wonderfully made:
Wonderful are thy works;
And that my soul knoweth right well.[1]

The Lord is my portion, saith my soul; therefore will I hope in him.
The Lord is good unto them that wait for him, to the soul that seeketh him.
It is good that a man should hope and quietly wait for the salvation of the Lord.
It is good for a man that he bear the yoke in his youth.
Let him sit alone and keep silence, because he hath laid it upon him.
Let him put his mouth in the dust; if so be there may be hope.
Let him give his cheek to him that smiteth him; let him be filled full with reproach.
   For the Lord will not cast off for ever.
For though he cause grief, yet will he have compassion according to the multitude of his mercies.
For he doth not afflict willingly, nor grieve the children of men.
To crush under foot all the prisoners of the earth,
To turn aside the right of a man before the face of the Most High,
To subvert a man in his cause, the Lord approveth not.
Who is he that saith, and it cometh to pass, when the Lord commandeth it not?

[1] Ps. 139: 1-14.

Out of the mouth of the Most High cometh there not
  evil and good?
Wherefore doth a living man complain, a man for the
  punishment of his sins?
  Let us search and try our ways, and turn again to
    the Lord.
Let us lift up our heart with our hands unto God in
  the heavens.[1]

Lord, my heart is not haughty, nor mine eyes lofty;
Neither do I exercise myself in great matters,
Or in things too wonderful for me.
Surely I have stilled and quieted my soul;
Like a weaned child with his mother,
My soul is with me like a weaned child.[2]

---

[1] Lam. 3: 24–41.   [2] Ps. 131: 1–2.

FIVE

THE GOD OF THE SPIRITS OF ALL FLESH[1]

> But there is a spirit in man,
> And the breath of the Almighty giveth them
> understanding.[2]

Some thinkers have told us that to recognise limitation (Section 4) is to overcome it; while others have said that the instinct for worship is part of the human make-up. We need not ask here whether the reaching out for perfection which in religion is the passion for God creates the object which satisfies it. For Biblical writers the question would be meaningless; and their conviction would be part of our own answer.

It is the character of that conviction as well as its strength which I have tried to illustrate in this Section. God seems to be apprehended as the source not only of time and space and physical things (as in Section 3) but also of personal integrity and right living.

O God, thou art my God ; early will I seek thee:
My soul thirsteth for thee, my flesh longeth for thee,
In a dry and weary land, where no water is.[3]

As the hart panteth after the water brooks,
So panteth my soul after thee, O God.
My soul thirsteth for God, for the living God:
When shall I come and appear before God?
   My tears have been my meat day and night,

---

[1] Num. 27: 16.   [2] Job. 32: 8.   [3] Ps. 63: 1.

While they continually say unto me, Where is thy God?
These things I remember, and pour out my soul within me,
How I went with the throng, and led them to the house of God,
With the voice of joy and praise, a multitude keeping holyday.
  Why art thou cast down, O my soul?
And why art thou disquieted within me?
Hope thou in God: for I shall yet praise him
For the health of his countenance.
  O my God, my soul is cast down within me:
Therefore do I remember thee from the land of Jordan,
And the Hermons, from the hill Mizar.
Deep calleth unto deep at the noise of thy waterspouts:
All thy waves and thy billows are gone over me.
Yet the Lord will command his lovingkindness in the day-time,
And in the night his song shall be with me,
Even a prayer unto the God of my life.
I will say unto God my rock, Why hast thou forgotten me?
Why go I mourning because of the oppression of the enemy?
As with a sword in my bones, mine adversaries reproach me;
While they continually say unto me,
Where is thy God?
  Why art thou cast down, O my soul?
And why art thou disquieted within me?
Hope thou in God: for I shall yet praise him,
Who is the health of my countenance, and my God.
  Judge me, O God, and plead my cause against an ungodly nation:
O deliver me from the deceitful and unjust man.

For thou art the God of my strength; why hast thou
  cast me off?
Why go I mourning because of the oppression of the
  enemy?
O send out thy light and thy truth; let them lead me:
Let them bring me unto thy holy hill,
And to thy tabernacles.
Then will I go unto the altar of God,
Unto God my exceeding joy:
And upon the harp will I praise thee, O God, my
  God.
Why art thou cast down, O my soul?
And why art thou disquieted within me?
Hope thou in God: for I shall yet praise him,
Who is the health of my countenance, and my God.[1]

Out of the depths have I cried unto thee, O Lord.
Lord, hear my voice:
Let thine ears be attentive
To the voice of my supplications.
If thou, Lord, shouldest mark iniquities,
O Lord, who shall stand?
But there is forgiveness with thee,
That thou mayest be feared.
I wait for the Lord, my soul doth wait,
And in his word do I hope.
My soul looketh for the Lord,
More than watchmen look for the morning;
Yea, more than watchmen for the morning.[2]

A Prayer of Moses the man of God.

Lord, thou hast been our dwelling place
In all generations.

[1] Ps. 42, 43.   [2] Ps. 130: 1–6.

Before the mountains were brought forth,
Or ever thou hadst formed the earth and the world,
Even from everlasting to everlasting, thou art God.
    Thou turnest man to destruction;
And sayest, Return, ye children of men.
For a thousand years in thy sight
Are but as yesterday when it is past,
And as a watch in the night.
Thou carriest them away as with a flood; they are as a sleep:
In the morning they are like grass which groweth up.
In the morning it flourisheth, and groweth up;
In the evening it is cut down, and withereth.
For we are consumed in thine anger,
And in thy wrath are we troubled.
    Thou hast set our iniquities before thee,
Our secret sins in the light of thy countenance.
For all our days are passed away in thy wrath:
We bring our years to an end as a tale that is told.
The days of our years are threescore years and ten,
Or even by reason of strength fourscore years;
Yet is their pride but labour and sorrow;
For it is soon gone, and we fly away.
    Who knoweth the power of thine anger,
And thy wrath according to the fear that is due unto thee?
So teach us to number our days,
That we may get us an heart of wisdom.
    Return, O Lord; how long?
And let it repent thee concerning thy servants.
O satisfy us in the morning with thy mercy;
That we may rejoice and be glad all our days.
Make us glad according to the days wherein thou hast afflicted us,
And the years wherein we have seen evil.

Let thy work appear unto thy servants,
And thy glory upon their children.
And let the beauty of the Lord our God be upon us:
And establish thou the work of our hands upon us;
Yea, the work of our hands establish thou it.[1]

And Joseph said unto his brethren, Come near to me, I pray you. And they came near. And he said, I am Joseph your brother, whom ye sold into Egypt.

And now be not grieved, nor angry with yourselves, that ye sold me hither, for God did send me before you to preserve life. For these two years hath the famine been in the land: and there are yet five years, in the which there shall be neither plowing nor harvest. And God sent me before you to preserve you a remnant in the earth, and to save you alive by a great deliverance.

So now it was not you that sent me hither, but God.[2]

I, even I, am he that comforteth you: who art thou, that thou art afraid of man that shall die, and of the son of man which shall be made as grass; and hast forgotten the Lord thy Maker.[3]

How art thou fallen from heaven, O day star, son of the morning! how art thou cut down to the ground, which didst lay low the nations!

And thou saidst in thine heart, I will ascend into heaven, I will exalt my throne above the stars of God; and I will sit upon the mount of congregation, in the uttermost parts of the north: I will ascend above the heights of the clouds; I will be like the Most High. Yet thou shalt be brought down to hell, to the uttermost parts of the pit.

[1]Ps. 90.   [2]Gen. 45: 4-8.   [3]Isa. 51: 12-13.

They that see thee shall narrowly look upon thee, they shall consider thee, saying, Is this the man that made the earth to tremble, that did shake kingdoms; that made the world as a wilderness, and overthrew the cities thereof; that let not loose his prisoners to their home?

All the kings of the nations, all of them, sleep in glory, every one in his own house. But thou art cast forth away from thy sepulchre like an abominable branch, clothed with the slain, that are thrust through with the sword, that go down to the stones of the pit; as a carcase trodden under foot.

Thou shalt not be joined with them in burial, because thou hast destroyed thy land, thou hast slain thy people.[1]

Now the Egyptians are men, and not God; and their horses flesh, and not spirit.[2]

Son of man, say unto the prince of Tyre, Thus saith the Lord God: Because thine heart is lifted up, and thou hast said, I am a god, I sit in the seat of God, in the midst of the seas; yet thou art man, and not God, though thou didst set thine heart as the heart of God: behold, thou art wiser than Daniel; there is no secret that they can hide from thee: by thy wisdom and by thine understanding thou hast gotten thee riches, and hast gotten gold and silver into thy treasures: by thy great wisdom and by thy traffic hast thou increased thy riches, and thine heart is lifted up because of thy riches.

Therefore thus saith the Lord God: Because thou hast set thine heart as the heart of God; therefore behold, I will bring strangers upon thee, the terrible of the nations: and they shall draw their swords against the

[1] Isa. 14: 12-20.   [2] Isa. 31: 3.

beauty of thy wisdom, and they shall defile thy brightness. They shall bring thee down to the pit; and thou shalt die the deaths of them that are slain, in the heart of the seas.

Wilt thou yet say before him that slayeth thee, I am God? but thou art man, and not God.[1]

For there shall be a day of the Lord of hosts upon all that is proud and haughty, and upon all that is lifted up; and it shall be brought low: and upon all the cedars of Lebanon, that are high and lifted up, and upon all the oaks of Bashan; and upon all the high mountains, and upon all the hills that are lifted up; and upon every lofty tower, and upon every fenced wall; and upon all the ships of Tarshish, and upon all pleasant imagery. And the loftiness of man shall be bowed down, and the haughtiness of men shall be brought low: and the Lord alone shall be exalted in that day. And the idols shall utterly pass away. And men shall go into the caves of the rocks, and into the holes of the earth, from before the terror of the Lord, and from the glory of his majesty, when he ariseth to shake mightily the earth.

In that day a man shall cast away his idols of silver, and his idols of gold, which they made for him to worship, to the moles and to the bats; to go into the caverns of the rocks, and into the clefts of the ragged rocks, from before the terror of the Lord, and from the glory of his majesty, when he ariseth to shake mightily the earth.

Cease ye from man, whose breath is in his nostrils: for wherein is he to be accounted of?[2]

Though thou mount on high as the eagle, and though thy nest be set among the stars, I will bring thee down from thence, saith the Lord.[3]

[1]Ezek. 28: 2–10.   [2]Isa. 2: 12–22.   [3]Obad. 1: 4.

O thou king, the Most High God gave Nebuchadnezzar thy father the kingdom, and greatness, and glory, and majesty: and because of the greatness that he gave him, all the peoples, nations, and languages trembled and feared before him: whom he would he slew, and whom he would he kept alive; and whom he would he raised up, and whom he would he put down.

But when his heart was lifted up, and his spirit was hardened that he dealt proudly, he was deposed from his kingly throne, and they took his glory from him: and he was driven from the sons of men; and his heart was made like the beasts, and his dwelling was with the wild asses; he was fed with grass like oxen, and his body was wet with the dew of heaven: until he knew that the Most High God ruleth in the kingdom of men, and that he setteth up over it whomsoever he will.

And thou his son, O Belshazzar, hast not humbled thine heart, though thou knewest all this; but hast lifted up thyself against the Lord of heaven; and they have brought the vessels of his house before thee, and thou and thy lords, thy wives and thy concubines, have drunk wine in them; and thou hast praised the gods of silver, and gold, of brass, iron, wood, and stone, which see not, nor hear, nor know: and the God in whose hand thy breath is, and whose are all thy ways, hast thou not glorified.

Then was the part of the hand sent from before him, and this writing was inscribed. And this is the writing that was inscribed, MENE, MENE, TEKEL, UPHARSIN.

This is the interpretation of the thing: MENE; God hath numbered thy kingdom, and brought it to an end. TEKEL; thou art weighed in the balances, and art found wanting. PERES; thy kingdom is divided, and given to the Medes and Persians.

Then commanded Belshazzar, and they clothed

Daniel with purple, and put a chain of gold about his neck, and made proclamation concerning him, that he should be the third ruler in the kingdom.

In that night Belshazzar the Chaldean king was slain.[1]

Who knoweth not in all these,
That the hand of the Lord hath wrought this?
In whose hand is the soul of every living thing,
And the breath of all mankind.[2]

With him is strength and effectual working;
The deceived and the deceiver are his.
He leadeth counsellors away spoiled,
And judges maketh he fools.
He looseth the bond of kings,
And bindeth their loins with a girdle.
He leadeth priests away spoiled,
And overthroweth the mighty.
He removeth the speech of the trusty,
And taketh away the understanding of the elders.
He poureth contempt upon princes,
And looseth the belt of the strong.
He discovereth deep things out of darkness,
And bringeth out to light the shadow of death.
He increaseth the nations, and destroyeth them:
He spreadeth the nations abroad, and bringeth them in.
He taketh away the heart of the chiefs of the people of the earth,
And causeth them to wander in a wilderness where there is no way.[3]

Am I a God at hand, saith the Lord, and not a God afar off? Can any hide himself in secret places that I

[1] Dan. 5: 18–30.   [2] Job 12: 9–10.   [3] Job 12: 16–24.

shall not see him? saith the Lord. Do not I fill heaven and earth? saith the Lord.[1]

There is no wisdom and there is no understanding and there is no counsel against the Lord.[2]

Which stretcheth forth the heavens, and layeth the foundation of the earth, and formeth the spirit of man within him.[3]

The spirit of man is the lamp of the Lord,
Searching all the innermost parts.[4]

The souls which I have made.[5]

If thou sayest, Behold, we knew not this:
   Doth not he that weigheth the hearts consider it?
And he that keepeth thy soul, doth not he know it?[6]

For man looketh on the outward appearance, but the Lord looketh on the heart.[7]

Thou, even thou only, knowest the hearts of all the children of men.[8]

Hear the causes between your brethren, and judge righteously between a man and his brother, and the stranger that is with him. Ye shall not respect persons in judgement; ye shall hear the small and the great alike; ye shall not be afraid of the face of man; for the judgement is God's.[9]

[1] Jer. 23: 23-24.
[2] Prov. 21: 30 (A).
[3] Zech. 12: 1.
[4] Prov. 21: 30.
[5] Isa. 57: 16.
[6] Prov. 24: 12.
[7] 1 Sam. 16: 7.
[8] 1 Kings 8: 39.
[9] Deut. 1: 16-17.

God standeth in the congregation of God;
In the midst of the judges he judgeth.[1]

I will not justify the wicked.[2]

Thou shalt not oppress an hired servant that is poor and needy, whether he be of thy brethren, or of thy strangers that are in thy land within thy gates: in his day thou shalt give him his hire, neither shall the sun go down upon it; for he is poor, and setteth his heart upon it.
  Lest he cry against thee unto the Lord, and it be sin unto thee.[3]

All my bones shall say, Lord, who is like unto thee,
Which deliverest the poor from him that is too strong
  for him,
Yea, the poor and the needy from him that spoileth
  him.[4]

The Lord of hosts is exalted in judgement, and God the Holy One is sanctified in righteousness.[5]

He that oppresseth the poor reproacheth his Maker:
But he that hath mercy on the needy honoureth him.[6]

I know that the Lord will maintain the cause of the
  afflicted,
And the right of the needy.[7]

Whoso mocketh the poor reproacheth his Maker.[8]

He that hath pity upon the poor lendeth unto the Lord.[9]

[1] Ps. 82: 1 (A).
[2] Exod. 23: 7.
[3] Deut. 24: 14–15.
[4] Ps. 35: 10.
[5] Isa. 5: 16.
[6] Prov. 14: 31.
[7] Ps. 140: 12.
[8] Prov. 17: 5.
[9] Prov. 19: 17.

In the day that God created man, in the likeness of
God made he him.[1]

The rich and the poor meet together:
The Lord is the maker of them all.[2]

Lord, I have called upon thee; make haste unto me:
Give ear unto my voice, when I call unto thee.
Let my prayer be set forth as incense before thee;
The lifting up of my hands as the evening sacrifice.
   Set a watch, O Lord, before my mouth;
Keep the door of my lips;
Incline not my heart to any evil thing.[3]

I delight to do thy will, O my God;
Yea, thy law is within my heart.[4]

The way of the just is uprightness: thou that art upright
dost direct the path of the just.[5]

Teach me to do thy will; for thou art my God:
Thy spirit is good; lead me in the land of uprightness.[6]

Thou triest the heart, and hast pleasure in uprightness.[7]

The upright shall dwell in thy presence.[8]

---

[1]Gen. 5: 1.
[2]Prov. 22: 2.
[3]Ps. 141: 1–4.
[4]Ps. 40: 8.
[5]Isa. 26: 7.
[6]Ps. 143: 10.
[7]1 Chron. 29: 17.
[8]Ps. 140: 13.

SIX

IN THEE I TRUST[1]

> In quietness and in confidence shall be your strength.[2]

Yet God is felt, not proven (unless the feeling constitutes the proof); and the feeling of Biblical writers was strong. The piety of the Psalmists was at times over-placid but it remains the very type of personal religion. Their God was their 'guide' not only 'unto death' but also, in some way they did not specify, beyond.

This God is our God for ever and ever:
He will be out guide even unto death.[3]

Thou wilt keep him in perfect peace, whose mind is stayed on thee: because he trusteth in thee.[4]

After these things the word of the Lord came unto Abram in a vision, saying, Fear not, Abram: I am thy shield, and thy exceeding great reward. And Abram said, O Lord God, what wilt thou give me, seeing I go childless, and he that shall be possessor of my house is Dammesek Eliezer? And Abram said, Behold, to me thou hast given no seed: and, lo, one born in my house is mine heir.

And, behold, the word of the Lord came unto him, saying, This man shall not be thine heir; but he that shall come forth out of thine own bowels shall be thine

---

[1] Ps. 143: 8.   [2] Isa. 30: 15.   [3] Ps. 48: 15.   [4] Isa. 26: 3.

heir. And he brought him forth abroad, and said, Look now toward heaven, and tell the stars, if thou be able to tell them: and he said unto him, So shall thy seed be.

And he believed in the Lord; and he counted it to him for righteousness.[1]

And David said to Saul, Let no man's heart fail because of him; thy servant will go and fight with this Philistine. And Saul said to David, Thou art not able to go against this Philistine to fight with him: for thou art but a youth, and he a man of war from his youth.

And David said unto Saul, Thy servant kept his father's sheep; and when there came a lion, or a bear, and took a lamb out of the flock, I went out after him, and smote him, and delivered it out of his mouth: and when he arose against me, I caught him by his beard, and smote him, and slew him. Thy servant smote both the lion and the bear; and this uncircumcised Philistine shall be as one of them, seeing he hath defied the armies of the living God.

And David said, The Lord that delivered me out of the paw of the lion, and out of the paw of the bear, he will deliver me out of the hand of this Philistine.[2]

A Psalm of David.

The Lord is my shepherd; I shall not want.
    He maketh me to lie down in green pastures:
He leadeth me beside the still waters.
He restoreth my soul:
He guideth me in the paths of righteousness for his
    name's sake.

[1]Gen. 15: 1–6. [2]1 Sam. 17: 32–37.

Yea, though I walk through the valley of the shadow
      of death,
I will fear no evil; for thou art with me:
Thy rod and thy staff, they comfort me.
Thou preparest a table before me in the presence of
      mine enemies:
Thou hast annointed my head with oil; my cup runneth
      over.
   Surely goodness and mercy shall follow me all the
      days of my life:
And I will dwell in the house of the Lord for ever.[1]

And he humbled thee, and suffered thee to hunger, and
fed thee with manna, which thou knewest not, neither
did thy fathers know; that he might make thee know
that man doth not live by bread only, but by every
thing that proceedeth out of the mouth of the Lord
doth man live.[2]

He that walketh in darkness, and hath no light, let
him trust in the name of the Lord, and stay upon his
God.[3]

The Lord is my light and my salvation; whom shall I
      fear?
The Lord is the strength of my life; of whom shall I be
      afraid?
When evil-doers came upon me to eat up my flesh,
Even mine adversaries and my foes, they stumbled and
      fell.
   Though an host should encamp against me,
My heart shall not fear:
Though war should rise against me,
Even then will I be confident.

[1] Ps. 23. [2] Deut. 8: 3. [3] Isa. 50: 10.

One thing have I asked of the Lord, that will I seek
    after;
That I may dwell in the house of the Lord all the days
    of my life,
To behold the beauty of the Lord, and to inquire in
    his temple.
  For in the day of trouble he shall keep me secretly
    in his pavilion:
In the covert of his tabernacle shall he hide me;
He shall lift me up upon a rock.
And now shall mine head be lifted up above mine
    enemies round about me;
And I will offer in his tabernacle sacrifices of joy;
I will sing, yea, I will sing praises unto the Lord.
  Hear, O Lord, when I cry with my voice:
Have mercy also upon me, and answer me.
When thou saidst, Seek ye my face; my heart said
    unto thee,
Thy face, Lord, will I seek.
  Hide not thy face from me;
Put not thy servant away in anger:
Thou hast been my help;
Cast me not off, neither forsake me, O God of my
    salvation.
For my father and mother have forsaken me,
But the Lord will take me up.
  Teach me thy way, O Lord;
And lead me in a plain path,
Because of mine enemies.
Deliver me not over unto the will of mine adversaries:
For false witnesses are risen up against me, and such
    as breathe out cruelty.
  I had fainted, unless I had believed to see the good-
    ness of the Lord
In the land of the living.

Wait on the Lord:
Be strong, and let thine heart take courage;
Yea, wait thou on the Lord.[1]

It is of the Lord's mercies that we are not consumed,
  because his compassions fail not.
They are new every morning; great is thy faithfulness.[2]

Therefore turn thou to thy God: keep mercy and judgement, and wait on thy God continually.[3]

The hand of our God is upon all them that seek him, for good.[4]

Now Naaman, captain of the host of the king of Syria, was a great man with his master, and honourable, because by him the Lord had given victory unto Syria: he was also a mighty man of valour, but he was a leper. And the Syrians had gone out in bands, and had brought away captive out of the land of Israel a little maid; and she waited on Naaman's wife. And she said unto her mistress, Would God my lord were with the prophet that is in Samaria! then would he recover him of his leprosy. And one went in, and told his lord, saying, Thus and thus said the maid that is of the land of Israel.

And the king of Syria said, Go to, go, and I will send a letter unto the king of Israel. And he departed, and took with him ten talents of silver, and six thousand pieces of gold, and ten changes of raiment. And he brought the letter to the king of Israel, saying, And now when this letter is come unto thee, behold, I have sent Naaman my servant to thee, that thou mayest

[1]Ps. 27.   [2]Lam. 3: 22-23.   [3]Hos. 12: 6.   [4]Ezra 8: 22.

recover him of his leprosy. And it came to pass, when the king of Israel had read the letter, that he rent his clothes, and said, Am I God, to kill and to make alive, that this man doth send unto me to recover a man of his leprosy? but consider, I pray you, and see how he seeketh a quarrel against me.

And it was so, when Elisha the man of God heard that the king of Israel had rent his clothes, that he sent to the king, saying, Wherefore hast thou rent thy clothes? let him come now to me, and he shall know that there is a prophet in Israel.

So Naaman came with his horses and with his chariots, and stood at the door of the house of Elisha. And Elisha sent a messenger unto him, saying, Go and wash in Jordan seven times, and thy flesh shall come again to thee, and thou shalt be clean.

But Naaman was wroth, and went away, and said, Behold, I thought, He will surely come out to me, and stand, and call on the name of the Lord his God, and wave his hand over the place, and recover the leper. Are not Abanah and Pharpar, the rivers of Damascus, better than all the waters of Israel? may I not wash in them, and be clean? So he turned and went away in a rage.

And his servants came near, and spake unto him, and said, My father, if the prophet had bid thee do some great thing, wouldest thou not have done it? how much rather then, when he saith to thee, Wash, and be clean?

Then went he down, and dipped himself seven times in Jordan, according to the saying of the man of God: and his flesh came again like unto the flesh of a little child, and he was clean.[1]

[1] 2 Kings 5: 1-14.

I will lift up mine eyes unto the mountains:
From whence shall my help come?
My help cometh from the Lord,
Which made heaven and earth.
He will not suffer thy foot to be moved:
He that keepeth thee will not slumber.
Behold, he that keepeth Israel
Shall neither slumber nor sleep.
   The Lord is thy keeper:
The Lord is thy shade upon thy right hand.
The sun shall not smite thee by day,
Nor the moon by night.
The Lord shall keep thee from all evil;
He shall keep thy soul.
The Lord shall keep thy going out and thy coming in,
From this time forth and for evermore.[1]

God is our refuge and strength,
A very present help in trouble.
Therefore will we not fear, though the earth do change,
And though the mountains be moved in the heart of
    the seas;
Though the waters thereof roar and be troubled,
Though the mountains shake with the swelling there-
    of.[2]   [Selah

They that go down to the sea in ships,
That do business in great waters;
These see the works of the Lord,
And his wonders in the deep.
For he commandeth, and raiseth the stormy wind,
Which lifteth up the waves thereof.
They mount up to the heaven, they go down again to
    the depths:

[1] Ps. 121.   [2] Ps. 46: 1-3.

Their soul melteth away because of trouble.
They reel to and fro, and stagger like a drunken man,
And are at their wits' end.
   Then they cry unto the Lord in their trouble,
And he bringeth them out of their distresses.
   He maketh the storm a calm,
So that the waves thereof are still.
Then they are glad because they be quiet;
So he bringeth them unto the haven where they would
   be.
   Oh that men would praise the Lord for his goodness,
And for his wonderful works to the children of men![1]

If ye will not believe, surely ye shall not be established.[2]

Be strong and of a good courage, be not afraid nor dismayed for the king of Assyria, nor for all the multitude that is with him: for there is a greater with us than with him: with him is an arm of flesh; but with us is the Lord our God.[3]

My soul, wait thou only upon God;
For my expectation is from him.
He only is my rock and my salvation:
He is my high tower; I shall not be moved.
With God is my salvation and my glory:
The rock of my strength, and my refuge, is in God.
   Trust in him at all times, ye people;
Pour out your heart before him:
God is a refuge for us.[4]   [Selah

The Lord is the portion of mine inheritance and of my
   cup:
Thou maintainest my lot.

[1] Ps. 107: 23–31.   [2] Isa. 7: 9.   [3] 2 Chron. 32: 7–8.   [4] Ps. 62: 5–8.

The lines are fallen unto me in pleasant places;
Yea, I have a goodly heritage.
I will bless the Lord, who hath given me counsel:
Yea, my reins instruct me in the night seasons.
I have set the Lord always before me:
Because he is at my right hand, I shall not be moved.
　Therefore my heart is glad, and my glory rejoiceth:
My flesh also shall dwell in safety.
For thou wilt not leave my soul to Sheol;
Neither wilt thou suffer thine holy one to see corruption.
　Thou wilt shew me the path of life:
In thy presence is fulness of joy;
In thy right hand there are pleasures for evermore.[1]

Nevertheless I am continually with thee:
Thou hast holden my right hand.
Thou shalt guide me with thy counsel,
And afterward receive me to glory.
　Whom have I in heaven but thee?
And there is none upon earth that I desire beside thee.
My flesh and my heart faileth:
But God is the strength of my heart and my portion for
　　ever.[2]

He that dwelleth in the secret place of the Most High
Shall abide under the shadow of the Almighty.
I will say of the Lord, He is my refuge and my fortress;
My God, in whom I trust.
For he shall deliver thee from the snare of the fowler,
And from the noisome pestilence.
He shall cover thee with his pinions,
And under his wings shalt thou take refuge:
His truth is a shield and a buckler.

[1] Ps. 16: 5-11.　　[2] Ps. 73: 23-26.

Thou shalt not be afraid for the terror by night,
Nor for the arrow that flieth by day;
For the pestilence that walketh in darkness,
Nor for the destruction that wasteth at noonday.
A thousand shall fall at thy side,
And ten thousand at thy right hand;
But it shall not come nigh thee.
Only with thine eyes shalt thou behold,
And see the reward of the wicked.
For thou, O Lord, art my refuge!
Thou hast made the Most High thy habitation.
There shall no evil befall thee,
Neither shall any plague come nigh thy tent.
For he shall give his angels charge over thee,
To keep thee in all thy ways.
They shall bear thee up in their hands,
Lest thou dash thy foot against a stone.
Thou shalt tread upon the lion and adder:
The young lion and the serpent shalt thou trample
  under feet.
Because he hath set his love upon me, therefore will I
  deliver him:
I will set him on high, because he hath known my name.
He shall call upon me, and I will answer him;
I will be with him in trouble:
I will deliver him, and honour him.
With long life will I satisfy him,
And shew him my salvation.[1]

As for me, I shall behold thy face in righteousness:
I shall be satisfied, when I awake, with thy likeness.[2]

I know that my redeemer liveth,
And that he shall stand up at the last upon the earth:

[1] Ps. 91.   [2] Ps. 17: 15.

And after my skin hath been thus destroyed,
Yet from my flesh shall I see God.[1]

Though he slay me, yet will I wait for him.[2]

With my soul have I desired thee in the night; yea, with my spirit within me will I seek thee early.[3]

When I awake, I am still with thee.[4]

With thee is the fountain of life:
In thy light shall we see light.[5]

I would know the words which he would answer me,
And understand what he would say unto me.
   Would he contend with me in the greatness of his power?
Nay; but he would give heed unto me.[6]

Men have not heard, nor perceived by the ear, neither hath the eye seen a God beside thee, which worketh for him that waiteth for him.
   Thou meetest him that rejoiceth and worketh righteousness, those that remember thee in thy ways.[7]

Search me, O God, and know my heart:
Try me, and know my thoughts:
And see if there be any way of wickedness in me,
And lead me in the way everlasting.[8]

---

[1] Job 19: 25–26.
[2] Job 13: 15.
[3] Isa. 26: 9.
[4] Ps. 139: 18.
[5] Ps. 36: 9.
[6] Job 23: 5–6.
[7] Isa. 64: 4–5.
[8] Ps. 139: 23–24.

SEVEN

THE PATH OF LIFE[1]

> I have set before thee life and death, the blessing and the curse: therefore choose life.[2]

In this Section I have collected passages containing summary rules of living. I have refrained from quoting some of the better known, and I have reserved the Ten Commandments for a Section (and 'commentary') of their own (8). One notes throughout the intense practicality of the demands made on man: even the divine ideal of Holiness is brought to earth by specific definition. At the same time the 'heart' is not forgotten. All action comes from disposition and purpose.

The constant call to 'righteousness' should not be misunderstood. The word itself seems to have gone out of modern usage and it has certainly lost its appeal. But the personal quality intended by it—it has been said to be 'the humanitarian virtue par excellence'—remains a primary requirement of morals. Righteousness is not to be confused with self-righteousness.

I am God Almighty; walk before me, and be thou perfect.[3]

These are the things that ye shall do; Speak ye every man the truth with his neighbour; execute the judgement of truth and peace in your gates: and let none of you imagine evil in your hearts against his neighbour; and love no false oath: for all these are things that I hate, saith the Lord.[4]

[1]Ps. 16: 11.   [2]Deut. 30: 19.   [3]Gen. 17: 1.   [4]Zech. 8: 16–17.

Lord, who shall sojourn in thy tabernacle?
Who shall dwell in thy holy hill?
   He that walketh uprightly, and worketh righteousness,
And speaketh truth in his heart.
He that slandereth not with his tongue,
Nor doeth evil to his friend,
Nor taketh up a reproach against his neighbour.
In whose eyes a reprobate is despised;
But he honoureth them that fear the Lord.
He that sweareth to his own hurt, and changeth not.
He that putteth not out his money to usury,
Nor taketh reward against the innocent.
   He that doeth these things shall never be moved.[1]

Wash you, make you clean; put away the evil of your doings from before mine eyes; cease to do evil: learn to do well; seek judgement, relieve the oppressed, judge the fatherless, plead for the widow.[2]

I delivered the poor that cried,
The fatherless also, that had none to help him.
The blessing of him that was ready to perish came upon me:
And I caused the widow's heart to sing for joy.
I put on righteousness, and it clothed me:
My justice was as a robe and a diadem.
I was eyes to the blind,
And feet was I to the lame.
I was a father to the needy:
And the cause of him that I knew not I searched out.[3]

Thus hath the Lord of hosts spoken, saying, Execute true judgement, and shew mercy and compassion every

[1] Ps. 15.   [2] Isa. 1: 16–17.   [3] Job 29: 12–16.

man to his brother: and oppress not the widow, nor the fatherless, the stranger, nor the poor; and let none of you imagine evil against his brother in your heart.[1]

Thou shalt not have in thy bag divers weights, a great and a small. Thou shalt not have in thine house divers measures, a great and a small.

A perfect and just weight shalt thou have; a perfect and just measure shalt thou have: that thy days may be long upon the land which the Lord thy God giveth thee. For all that do such things, even all that do unrighteously, are an abomination unto the Lord thy God.[2]

Thou shalt not abhor an Edomite; for he is thy brother.

Thou shalt not abhor an Egyptian; because thou wast a stranger in his land.[3]

And Ben-hadad fled, and came into the city, into an inner chamber And his servants said unto him, Behold now, we have heard that the kings of the house of Israel are merciful kings: let us, we pray thee, put sackcloth on our loins, and ropes upon our heads, and go out to the king of Israel: peradventure he will save thy life. So they girded sackcloth on their loins, and put ropes on their heads, and came to the king of Israel, and said, Thy servant Ben-hadad saith, I pray thee, let me live. And he said, Is he yet alive? he is my brother.

Now the men observed diligently, and hasted to catch whether it were his mind; and they said, Thy brother Ben-hadad.

Then he said, Go ye, bring him. Then Ben-hadad came forth to him; and he caused him to come up

---

[1] Zech. 7: 9-10.   [2] Deut. 25: 13-16.   [3] Deut. 23: 7.

into the chariot. And Ben-hadad said unto him, The cities which my father took from thy father I will restore; and thou shalt make streets for thee in Damascus, as my father made in Samaria.
And I, said Ahab, will let thee go with this covenant. So he made a covenant with him, and let him go.[1]

When thou shalt besiege a city a long time, in making war against it to take it, thou shalt not destroy the trees thereof by wielding an axe against them; for thou mayest eat of them, and thou shalt not cut them down; for is the tree of the field man, that it should be besieged of thee?[2]

If thine enemy be hungry, give him bread to eat;
And if he be thirsty, give him water to drink.[3]

And the king of Israel said unto Elisha, when he saw them, My father, shall I smite them? shall I smite them? And he answered, Thou shalt not smite them.
Wouldest thou smite those whom thou hast taken captive with thy sword and with thy bow? set bread and water before them, that they may eat and drink.[4]

If a bird's nest chance to be before thee in the way, in any tree or on the ground, with young ones or eggs, and the dam sitting upon the young, or upon the eggs, thou shalt not take the dam with the young.[5]

Thou shalt not plow with an ox and an ass together.[6]

Thou shalt not muzzle the ox when he treadeth out the corn.[7]

[1] 1 Kings 20: 30-34. [2] Deut. 20: 19. [3] Prov. 25: 21. [4] 2 Kings 6: 21-22. [5] Deut. 22: 6. [6] Deut. 22: 10. [7] Deut. 25: 4.

And ye shall be holy men unto me: therefore ye shall not eat any flesh that is torn of beasts in the field; ye shall cast it to the dogs.[1]

For I am the Lord that brought you up out of the land of Egypt, to be your God: ye shall therefore be holy, for I am holy.[2]

Thou shalt have a place also without the camp, whither thou shalt go forth abroad: and thou shalt have a paddle among thy weapons; and it shall be, when thou sittest down abroad, thou shalt dig therewith, and shalt turn back and cover that which cometh from thee: for the Lord thy God walketh in the midst of thy camp, to deliver thee, and to give up thine enemies before thee; therefore shall thy camp be holy.[3]

And thou shalt not defile the land which ye inhabit, in the midst of which I dwell: for I the Lord dwell in the midst of the children of Israel.[4]

Trust ye not in lying words, saying, The temple of the Lord, the temple of the Lord, the temple of the Lord, are these.
    For [only] if ye thoroughly amend your ways and your doings; if ye thoroughly execute judgement between a man and his neighbour; if ye oppress not the stranger, the fatherless, and the widow, and shed not innocent blood in this place, neither walk after other gods to your own hurt: [only] then will I cause you to dwell in this place, in the land that I gave to your fathers, from of old even for evermore.[5]

[1]Exod. 22: 31.   [3]Deut. 23: 12–14.   [5]Jer. 7: 4–7.
[2]Lev. 11: 45.   [4]Num. 35: 34.

They shall not hurt nor destroy in all my holy mountain, saith the Lord.[1]

Ye shall be holy: for I the Lord your God am holy. Ye shall fear every man his mother, and his father, and ye shall keep my sabbaths: I am the Lord your God.

Turn ye not unto idols, nor make to yourselves molten gods: I am the Lord your God. . . .

And when ye reap the harvest of your land, thou shalt not wholly reap the corners of thy field, neither shalt thou gather the gleaning of thy harvest. And thou shalt not glean thy vineyard, neither shalt thou gather the fallen fruit of thy vineyard; thou shalt leave them for the poor and for the stranger: I am the Lord your God.

Ye shall not steal; neither shall ye deal falsely, nor lie to one another. And ye shall not swear by my name falsely, so that thou profane the name of thy God: I am the Lord.

Thou shalt not oppress thy neighbour, nor rob him: the wages of a hired servant shall not abide with thee all night until the morning. Thou shalt not curse the deaf, nor put a stumblingblock before the blind, but thou shalt fear thy God: I am the Lord.

Ye shall do no unrighteousness in judgement: thou shalt not respect the person of the poor, nor honour the person of the mighty: but in righteousness shalt thou judge thy neighbour. Thou shalt not go up and down as a talebearer among thy people: neither shalt thou stand against the blood of thy neighbour: I am the Lord.

Thou shalt not hate thy brother in thine heart: thou shalt surely rebuke thy neighbour, and not bear sin because of him. Thou shalt not take vengeance, nor

[1] Isa. 65: 25.

bear any grudge against the children of thy people, but thou shalt love thy neighbour as thyself: I am the Lord.[1]

When thou dost lend thy neighbour any manner of loan, thou shalt not go into his house to fetch his pledge. Thou shalt stand without, and the man to whom thou dost lend shall bring forth the pledge without unto thee.
And if he be a poor man, thou shalt not sleep with his pledge: thou shalt surely restore to him the pledge when the sun goeth down, that he may sleep in his garment, and bless thee: and it shall be righteousness unto thee before the Lord thy God.[2]

Thou shalt not see thy brother's ox or his sheep go astray, and hide thyself from them: thou shalt surely bring them again unto thy brother. And if thy brother be not nigh unto thee, or if thou know him not, then thou shalt bring it home to thine house, and it shall be with thee until thy brother seek after it, and thou shalt restore it to him again. And so shalt thou do with his ass; and so shalt thou do with his garment; and so shalt thou do with every lost thing of thy brother's, which he hath lost, and thou hast found: thou mayest not hide thyself.
Thou shalt not see thy brother's ass or his ox fallen down by the way, and hide thyself from them: thou shalt surely help him to lift them up again.[3]

Thou shalt not take up a false report: put not thine hand with the wicked to be an unrighteous witness. Thou shalt not follow a multitude to do evil; neither shalt thou speak in a cause to turn aside after a

[1] Lev. 19: 2-4, 9-18.   [2] Deut. 24: 10-13.   [3] Exod. 22: 1-4.

multitude to wrest judgement: neither shalt thou favour a poor man in his cause.

If thou meet thine enemy's ox or his ass going astray, thou shalt surely bring it back to him again. If thou see the ass of him that hateth thee lying under his burden, and wouldest forbear to help him, thou shalt surely help with him.

Thou shalt not wrest the judgement of thy poor in his cause. Keep thee far from a false matter; and the innocent and righteous slay thou not.[1]

If I did despise the cause of my manservant or of my maidservant,
When they contended with me:
What then shall I do when God riseth up?
And when he visiteth, what shall I answer him?
Did not he that made me in the womb make him?
And did not one fashion us in the womb?
    If I have withheld the poor from their desire,
Or have caused the eyes of the widow to fail;
Or have eaten my morsel alone,
And the fatherless hath not eaten thereof;
(Nay, from my youth he grew up with me as with a father,
And I have been her guide from my mother's womb;)
    If I have seen any perish for want of clothing,
Or that the needy had no covering;
If his loins have not blessed me,
And if he were not warmed with the fleece of my sheep;
    If I have lifted up my hand against the fatherless,
Because I saw my help in the gate:
Then let my shoulder fall from the shoulder blade,
And mine arm be broken from the bone.

[1] Exod. 23: 1–7.

For calamity from God was a terror to me,
And by reason of his excellency I could do nothing.
   If I have made gold my hope,
And have said to the fine gold, Thou art my confidence;
If I rejoiced because my wealth was great,
And because mine hand had gotten much;
If I beheld the sun when it shined,
Or the moon walking in brightness;
And my heart hath been secretly enticed,
And my mouth hath kissed my hand:
This also were an iniquity to be punished by the judges:
For I should have lied to God that is above.
   If I rejoiced at the destruction of him that hated me,
Or lifted up myself when evil found him;
(Yea, I suffered not my mouth to sin
By asking his life with a curse;)
If the men of my tent said not,
Who can find one that hath not been satisfied with his flesh?
The stranger did not lodge in the street;
But I opened my doors to the traveller.[1]

Thou shalt not deliver unto his master a servant which is escaped from his master unto thee.[2]

Hide the outcasts; bewray not the wanderer.[3]

Seek good, and not evil, that ye may live: and so the Lord, the God of hosts, shall be with you, as ye say.
   Hate the evil, and love the good, and establish judgement in the gate.[4]

Let judgement roll down as waters, and righteousness as a mighty stream.[5]

[1] Job 31: 13–32. [3] Isa. 16: 3. [5] Amos 5: 24.
[2] Deut. 23: 15 [4] Amos 5: 14–15.

What man is he that desireth life,
And loveth many days, that he may see good?
Keep thy tongue from evil,
And thy lips from speaking guile.[1]

Amend your ways and your doings.[2]

Seek righteousness, seek meekness.[3]

Rend your heart, and not your garments.[4]

Consider your ways.[5]

Whatsoever thy hand findeth to do, do it with thy might.[6]

Open thy mouth for the dumb,
In the cause of all such as are left desolate.
Open thy mouth, judge righteously,
And minister judgement to the poor and needy.[7]

Love truth and peace.[8]

Seek peace, and pursue it.[9]

Thou shalt not revile the gods [of other people].[10]

Two things have I asked of thee;
Deny me them not before I die:
Remove far from me vanity and lies:
Give me neither poverty nor riches.[11]

[1] Ps. 34: 12–13.
[2] Jer. 7: 3.
[3] Zeph. 2: 3.
[4] Joel 2: 13.
[5] Hag. 1: 5.
[6] Eccles. 9: 10.
[7] Prov. 31: 8–9.
[8] Zech. 8: 19.
[9] Ps. 34: 14.
[10] Exod. 22: 28 (A)— an early rendering.
[11] Prov. 30: 7–8.

In that night did God appear unto Solomon, and said unto him, Ask what I shall give thee. And Solomon said unto God, Thou hast shewed great kindness unto David my father, and hast made me king in his stead. Now, O Lord God, let thy promise unto David my father be established: for thou hast made me king over a people like the dust of the earth in multitude. Give me now wisdom and knowledge that I may go out and come in before this people: for who can judge this thy people, that is so great? And God said to Solomon, Because this was in thine heart, and thou hast not asked riches, wealth, or honour, nor the life of them that hate thee, neither yet hast asked long life; but hast asked wisdom and knowledge for thyself, that thou mayest judge my people, over whom I have made thee king: wisdom and knowledge is granted unto thee; and I will give thee riches, and wealth, and honour.[1]

Go thy way, eat thy bread with joy, and drink thy wine with a merry heart.[2]

Cry aloud, spare not, lift up thy voice like a trumpet, and declare unto my people their transgression, and to the house of Jacob their sins. Yet they seek me daily, and delight to know my ways: as a nation that did righteousness, and forsook not the ordinance of their God, they ask of me righteous ordinances, they delight to draw near unto God. Wherefore have we fasted, say they, and thou seest not? wherefore have we afflicted our soul, and thou takest no knowledge? Behold, in the day of your fast ye find your own pleasure, and exact all your labours.

[1] 2 Chron. 1: 7–12.   [2] Eccles. 9: 7.

Behold, ye fast for strife and contention, and to smite with the fist of wickedness: ye fast not this day so as to make your voice to be heard on high.

Is such the fast that I have chosen? the day for a man to afflict his soul? Is it to bow down his head as a rush, and to spread sackcloth and ashes under him? wilt thou call this a fast, and an acceptable day to the Lord?

Is not this the fast that I have chosen? to loose the bonds of wickedness, to undo the bands of the yoke, and to let the oppressed go free, and that ye break every yoke? Is it not to deal thy bread to the hungry, and that thou bring the poor that are cast out to thy house? when thou seest the naked, that thou cover him; and that thou hide not thyself from thine own flesh?

Then shall thy light break forth as the morning, and thy healing shall spring forth speedily: and thy righteousness shall go before thee; the glory of the Lord shall be thy rearward. Then shalt thou call, and the Lord shall answer; thou shalt cry, and he shall say, Here I am.[1]

The Lord is with you, while ye be with him; and if ye seek him, he will be found of you; but if ye forsake him, he will forsake you.[2]

Who shall ascend into the hill of the Lord?
And who shall stand in his holy place?
He that hath clean hands, and a pure heart;
Who hath not lifted up his soul unto vanity,
And hath not sworn deceitfully.[3]

[1] Isa. 58: 1-9.   [2] Chron. 15: 2.   [3] Ps. 24: 3-4.

He that walketh righteously, and speaketh uprightly; he that despiseth the gain of oppressions, that shaketh his hands from holding of bribes, that stoppeth his ears from hearing of blood, and shutteth his eyes from looking upon evil; he shall dwell on high.[1]

---

[1] Isa. 33: 15-16.

EIGHT

THE TEN WORDS[1]

> For this commandment which I command thee this day, it is not too hard for thee, neither is it far off.
> It is not in heaven, that thou shouldest say, Who shall go up for us to heaven, and bring it unto us, and make us to hear it, that we may do it? Neither is it beyond the sea, that thou shouldest say, Who shall go over the sea for us, and bring it unto us, and make us to hear it, that we may do it?
> But the word is very nigh unto thee, in thy mouth, and in thy heart, that thou mayest do it.[2]

The point of this Section is that the 'ten commandments' (in Hebrew, the Ten Words) are not isolated proclamations; they are one with the whole stream of Biblical ethics. And they constitute moral claims. Even the first Word is no bare transcendental pronouncement or historical asseveration but, as the 'commentary' shows, a living lesson in practical morals: it is meant for our own application in our own conduct.

Recent scholars are fond of saying that the original ten commandments are not these but a ritual decalogue discoverable (with some difficulty) in another chapter. If this were so, it would only serve to throw into clearer light the nature of our debt to the Hebrew Bible; for it would involve the further and most significant point that the ritual decalogue was consciously suppressed in favour of the moral one: God 'requires mercy (i.e., 'steadfast love', as the Revised Standard Version translates), not sacrifice'.

[1]Deut. 4: 13 (M).   [2]Deut. 30: 11-14.

I have put the last five together because the Biblical narrative, like social experience, shows that all types of ill-doing go together. But no one of the Words is in fact detachable from the rest. They all involve one another and flow into one another in the wholeness of the moral life and the integrity of the moral personality.

I AM THE LORD THY GOD, WHICH BROUGHT THEE OUT OF THE LAND OF EGYPT, OUT OF THE HOUSE OF BONDAGE.[1]

Ye shall do no unrighteousness in judgement, in meteyard, in weight, or in measure. Just balances, just weights, a just ephah, and a just hin, shall ye have: I am the Lord your God, which brought you out of the land of Egypt.[2]

Thou shalt not wrest the judgement of the stranger, nor of the fatherless; nor take the widow's raiment to pledge: but thou shalt remember that thou wast a bondman in Egypt, and the Lord thy God redeemed thee thence; therefore I command thee to do this thing.[3]

And a stranger shalt thou not wrong, neither shalt thou oppress him: for ye were strangers in the land of Egypt.[4]

And if a stranger sojourn with thee in your land, ye shall not do him wrong. The stranger that sojourneth with you shall be unto you as the homeborn among you, and thou shalt love him as thyself; for ye were strangers in the land of Egypt: I am the Lord your God.[5]

[1] Exod. 20: 2.
[2] Lev. 19: 35–36.
[3] Deut. 24: 17–18.
[4] Exod. 22: 21.
[5] Lev. 19: 33–34.

Love ye therefore the stranger: for ye were strangers in the land of Egypt.[1]

And a stranger thou shalt not oppress: for ye know the heart of a stranger, seeing ye were strangers in the land of Egypt.[2]

When thou beatest thine olive tree, thou shalt not go over the boughs again: it shall be for the stranger, for the fatherless, and for the widow. When thou gatherest the grapes of thy vineyard, thou shalt not glean it after thee: it shall be for the stranger, for the fatherless, and for the widow.
 And thou shalt remember that thou wast a bondman in the land of Egypt: therefore I command thee to do this thing.[3]

Thy manservant and thy maidservant may rest as well as thou.
 And thou shalt remember that thou wast a servant in the land of Egypt, and the Lord thy God brought thee out thence.[4]

If thy brother, an Hebrew man, or an Hebrew woman, be sold unto thee, and serve thee six years; then in the seventh year thou shalt let him go free from thee. And when thou lettest him go free from thee, thou shalt not let him go empty: thou shalt furnish him liberally out of thy flock, and out of thy threshing-floor, and out of thy winepress: as the Lord thy God hath blessed thee thou shalt give unto him.
 And thou shalt remember that thou wast a bondman in the land of Egypt, and the Lord thy God redeemed thee: therefore I command thee this thing to-day.[5]

[1]Deut. 10: 19.
[2]Exod. 23: 9.
[3]Deut. 24: 20–22.
[4]Deut. 5: 14–15.
[5]Deut. 15: 12–15.

And if thy brother be waxen poor, and his hand fail with thee;, then thou shalt uphold him: as a stranger and a sojourner shall he live with thee. Take thou no usury of him or increase; but fear thy God: that thy brother may live with thee. Thou shalt not give him thy money upon usury, nor give him thy victuals for increase.

I am the Lord your God, which brought you forth out of the land of Egypt, to give you the land of Canaan, to be your God.[1]

And if thy brother be waxen poor with thee, and sell himself unto thee; thou shalt not make him to serve as a bondservant: as an hired servant, and as a sojourner, he shall be with thee; he shall serve with thee unto the year of jubile: then shall he go out from thee, he and his children with him, and shall return unto his own family, and unto the possession of his fathers shall he return.

For they are my servants, which I brought forth out of the land of Egypt: they shall not be sold as bondmen.[2]

Unto me the children of Israel are servants; they are my servants whom I brought forth out of the land of Egypt: I am the Lord your God.[3]

I will walk among you, and will be your God, and ye shall be my people. I am the Lord your God, which brought you forth out of the land of Egypt, that ye should not be their bondmen; and I have broken the bars of your yoke, and made you go upright.[4]

The Lord hath anointed me to preach good tidings unto the poor; he hath sent me to bind up the broken-

---

[1] Lev. 25: 35–38.   [2] Lev. 25: 39–42.   [3] Lev. 25: 55.   [4] Lev. 26: 12–13.

hearted, to proclaim liberty to the captives, and the opening of the prison to them that are bound.[1]

To open the blind eyes, to bring out the prisoners from the dungeon, and them that sit in darkness out of the prison house.
 I am the Lord; that is my name; and my glory will I not give to another, neither my praise unto graven images.[2]

THOU SHALT HAVE NONE OTHER GODS BEFORE ME. THOU SHALT NOT MAKE UNTO THEE A GRAVEN IMAGE, NOR THE LIKENESS OF ANY FORM THAT IS IN HEAVEN ABOVE, OR THAT IS IN THE EARTH BENEATH, OR THAT IS IN THE WATER UNDER THE EARTH: THOU SHALT NOT BOW DOWN THYSELF UNTO THEM, NOR SERVE THEM.[3]

And he said unto them, I am an Hebrew; and I fear the Lord, the God of heaven, which hath made the sea and the dry land.[4]

After these things did king Ahasuerus promote Haman the son of Hammedatha the Agagite, and advanced him, and set his seat above all the princes that were with him. And all the king's servants, that were in the king's gate, bowed down, and did reverence to Haman: for the king had so commanded concerning him.
 But Mordecai bowed not down.[5]

At that time certain Chaldeans came near, and brought accusation against the Jews.
 They answered and said to Nebuchadnezzar the king, O king, live for ever. Thou, O king, hast made a

[1]Isa. 61: 1 (m). [3]Exod. 20: 3–5. [5]Esther 3: 1–2.
[2]Isa. 42: 7–8. [4]Jonah 1: 9.

decree, that every man that shall hear the sound of the cornet, flute, harp, sackbut, psaltery, and dulcimer, and all kinds of music, shall fall down and worship the golden image: and whoso falleth not down and worshippeth, shall be cast into the midst of a burning fiery furnace. There are certain Jews whom thou hast appointed over the affairs of the province of Babylon, Shadrach, Meshach, and Abed-nego; these men, O king, have not regarded thee: they serve not thy gods, nor worship the golden image which thou hast set up.

Then Nebuchadnezzar in his rage and fury commanded to bring forth Shadrach, Meshach, and Abed-nego. Then they brought these men before the king.

Nebuchadnezzar answered and said unto them, Is it of purpose, O Shadrach, Meshach, and Abed-nego, that ye serve not my god, nor worship the golden image which I have set up? Now if ye be ready that at what time ye hear the sound of the cornet, flute, harp, sackbut, psaltery, and dulcimer, and all kinds of music, ye fall down and worship the image which I have made, well: but if ye worship not, ye shall be cast the same hour into the midst of a burning fiery furnace; and who is that god that shall deliver you out of my hands?

Shadrach, Meshach, and Abed-nego, answered and said to the king, O Nebuchadnezzar, we have no need to answer thee in this matter. If our God whom we serve be able to deliver us, he will deliver us from the burning fiery furnace and out of thine hand, O king.

But if not, be it known to thee, O king, that we will not serve thy gods, nor worship the golden image which thou hast set up.[1]

What profiteth the graven image, that the maker thereof hath graven it; the molten image, and the

[1] Dan. 3: 8-18 (M).

teacher of lies, that the maker of his work trusteth therein, to make dumb idols?

Woe unto him that saith to the wood, Awake: to the dumb stone, Arise! Shall this teach? Behold, it is laid over with gold and silver, and there is no breath at all in the midst of it.[1]

The smith maketh an axe, and worketh in the coals, and fashioneth it with hammers, and worketh it with his strong arm: yea, he is hungry, and his strength faileth; he drinketh no water, and is faint. The carpenter stretcheth out a line; he marketh it out with a pencil; he shapeth it with planes, and he marketh it out with the compasses, and shapeth it after the figure of a man, according to the beauty of a man, to dwell in the house. He heweth him down cedars, and taketh the holm tree and the oak, and strengtheneth for himself one among the trees of the forest: he planteth a fir tree, and the rain doth nourish it. Then shall it be for a man to burn; and he taketh thereof, and warmeth himself; yea, he kindleth it, and baketh bread; yea, he maketh a god, and worshippeth it; he maketh it a graven image, and falleth down thereto.

He burneth part thereof in the fire; with part thereof he eateth flesh; he roasteth roast, and is satisfied: yea, he warmeth himself, and saith, Aha, I am warm, I have seen the fire: and the residue thereof he maketh a god, even his graven image: he falleth down unto it and worshippeth, and prayeth unto it, and saith, Deliver me; for thou art my god.[2]

So Ahab sent unto all the children of Israel, and gathered the prophets together unto mount Carmel.

And Elijah came near unto all the people, and said,

[1]Hab. 2: 18-19.   [2]Isa. 44: 12-17.

How long halt ye between two opinions? if the Lord be God, follow him: but if Baal, then follow him. And the people answered him not a word.

Then said Elijah unto the people, I, even I only, am left a prophet of the Lord; but Baal's prophets are four hundred and fifty men. Let them therefore give us two bullocks; and let them choose one bullock for themselves, and cut it in pieces, and lay it on the wood, and put no fire under: and I will dress the other bullock, and lay it on the wood, and put no fire under. And call ye on the name of your god, and I will call on the name of the Lord: and the God that answereth by fire, let him be God. And all the people answered and said, It is well spoken.

And Elijah said unto the prophets of Baal, Choose you one bullock for yourselves, and dress it first; for ye are many; and call on the name of your god, but put no fire under. And they took the bullock which was given them, and they dressed it, and called on the name of Baal from morning even until noon, saying, O Baal, hear us. But there was no voice, nor any that answered. And they leaped about the altar which was made.

And it came to pass at noon, that Elijah mocked them, and said, Cry aloud: for he is a god; either he is musing, or he is gone aside, or he is in a journey, or peradventure he sleepeth, and must be awaked. And they cried aloud, and cut themselves after their manner with knives and lances, till the blood gushed out upon them. And it was so, when midday was past, that they prophesied until the time of the offering of the evening oblation; but there was neither voice, nor any to answer, nor any that regarded.

And Elijah said unto all the people, Come near unto me; and all the people came near unto him. And he repaired the altar of the Lord that was thrown down.

And Elijah took twelve stones, according to the number of the tribes of the sons of Jacob, unto whom the word of the Lord came, saying, Israel shall by thy name. And with the stones he built an altar in the name of the Lord; and he made a trench about the altar, as great as would contain two measures of seed. And he put the wood in order, and cut the bullock in pieces, and laid it on the wood. And he said, Fill four barrels with water, and pour it on the burnt offering, and on the wood. And he said, Do it the second time; and they did it the second time. And he said, Do it the third time; and they did it the third time. And the water ran round about the altar; and he filled the trench also with water.

And it came to pass at the time of the offering of the evening oblation, that Elijah the prophet came near, and said, O Lord, the God of Abraham, of Isaac, and of Israel, let it be known this day that thou art God in Israel, and that I am thy servant, and that I have done all these things at thy word. Hear me, O Lord, hear me, that this people may know that thou, Lord, art God, and that thou hast turned their heart back again.

Then the fire of the Lord fell, and consumed the burnt offering, and the wood, and the stones, and the dust, and licked up the water that was in the trench. And when all the people saw it, they fell on their faces: and they said, The Lord, he is God; the Lord, he is God.[1]

Not unto us, O Lord, not unto us,
But unto thy name give glory,
For thy mercy, and for thy truth's sake.
Wherefore should the nations say,
Where is now their God?

[1] 1 Kings 18: 20-39.

But our God is in the heavens:
He hath done whatsoever he pleased.
   Their idols are silver and gold,
The work of men's hands.
They have mouths, but they speak not;
Eyes have they, but they see not;
They have ears, but they hear not;
Noses have they, but they smell not;
They have hands, but they handle not;
Feet have they, but they walk not;
Neither speak they through their throat.
   They that make them shall be like unto them;
Yea, every one that trusteth in them.[1]

But the Lord is God in truth; he is the living God, and an everlasting king: at his wrath the earth trembleth, and the nations are not able to abide his indignation. Thus shall ye say unto them, The gods that have not made the heavens and the earth, they shall perish from the earth, and from under these heavens.[2]

He who blesseth himself in the earth shall bless himself in the God of truth; and he that sweareth in the earth shall swear by the God of truth.[3]

The king shall rejoice in God:
Every one that sweareth by him shall glory;
For the mouth of them that speak lies shall be stopped.[4]

THOU SHALT NOT TAKE THE NAME OF THE LORD THY GOD IN VAIN.[5]

O Lord our God, other lords beside thee have had dominion over us; but by thee only will we make

---

[1] Ps. 115: 1–10.
[2] Jer. 10: 10–11 (M).
[3] Isa. 65: 16.
[4] Ps. 63: 11.
[5] Exod. 20: 7.

mention of thy name. They are dead, they shall not live; they are deceased, they shall not rise.[1]

I lifted up mine eyes, and saw, and behold, a flying roll. And he said unto me, What seest thou? And I answered, I see a flying roll; the length thereof is twenty cubits, and the breadth thereof ten cubits. Then saith he unto me, This is the curse that goeth forth over the face of the whole land: for every one that stealeth shall be purged out on the one side according to it; and every one that sweareth shall be purged out on the other side according to it.

I will cause it to go forth, saith the Lord of hosts, and it shall enter into the house of the thief, and into the house of him that sweareth falsely by my name: and it shall abide in the midst of his house, and shall consume it with the timber thereof and the stones thereof.[2]

When a man voweth a vow unto the Lord, or sweareth an oath to bind his soul with a bond, he shall not break his word; he shall do according to all that proceedeth out of his mouth.[3]

When thou vowest a vow unto God, defer not to pay it; for he hath no pleasure in fools: pay that which thou vowest. Better is it that thou shouldest not vow, than that thou shouldest vow and not pay.[4]

If thou shalt forbear to vow, it shall be no sin in thee.
That which is gone out of thy lips thou shalt observe and do.[5]

[1]Isa. 26: 13–14.
[2]Zech. 5: 1–4.
[3]Num. 30: 2.
[4]Eccels. 5: 4–5.
[5]Deut. 23: 22–23.

Moreover the word of the Lord came unto me, saying, Say now to the rebellious house, Know ye not what these things mean? tell them, Behold, the king of Babylon came to Jerusalem, and took the king thereof, and the princes thereof, and brought them to him to Babylon; and he took of the seed royal, and made a covenant with him; he also brought him under an oath, and took away the mighty of the land: that the kingdom might be base, that it might not lift itself up, but that by keeping of his covenant it might stand.

But he rebelled against him in sending his ambassadors into Egypt, that they might give him horses and much people. Shall he prosper? shall he escape that doeth such things? shall he break the covenant, and yet escape? As I live, saith the Lord God, surely in the place where the king dwelleth that made him king, whose oath he despised, and whose covenant he brake, even with him in the midst of Babylon he shall die. Neither shall Pharaoh with his mighty army and great company make for him in the war, when they cast up mounts and build forts, to cut off many persons.

For he hath despised the oath by breaking the covenant; and behold, he had given his hand, and yet hath done all these things; he shall not escape. Therefore thus saith the Lord God: As I live, surely mine oath that he hath despised, and my covenant that he hath broken, I will even bring it upon his own head. And I will spread my net upon him, and he shall be taken in my snare, and I will bring him to Babylon, and will plead with him there for his trespass that he hath trespassed against Me.[1]

Thou shalt swear, As the Lord liveth, in truth, in judgement, and in righteousness; and the nations

---

[1] Ezek. 17: 11-20.

shall bless themselves in him, and in him shall they glory.[1]

Thus saith the Lord, Keep ye judgement, and do righteousness: for my salvation is near to come, and my righteousness to be revealed. Blessed is the man that doeth this, and the son of man that holdeth fast by it; that keepeth the sabbath from profaning it, and keepeth his hand from doing any evil.[2]

REMEMBER THE SABBATH DAY, TO KEEP IT HOLY. SIX DAYS SHALT THOU LABOUR, AND DO ALL THY WORK: BUT THE SEVENTH DAY IS A SABBATH UNTO THE LORD THY GOD: IN IT THOU SHALT NOT DO ANY WORK, THOU, NOR THY SON, NOR THY DAUGHTER, THY MANSERVANT, NOR THY MAIDSERVANT, NOR THY CATTLE, NOR THY STRANGER THAT IS WITHIN THY GATES.[3]

And the heaven and the earth were finished, and all the host of them. And on the seventh day God finished his work which he had made; and he rested on the seventh day from all his work which he had made. And God blessed the seventh day, and hallowed it: because that in it he rested from all his work which God had created and made.[4]

Observe the sabbath day, to keep it holy, as the Lord thy God commanded thee. Six days shalt thou labour, and do all thy work: but the seventh day is a sabbath unto the Lord thy God; in it thou shalt not do any work, thou, nor thy son, nor thy daughter, nor thy manservant, nor thy maidservant, nor thine ox, nor thine ass, nor any of thy cattle, nor thy stranger that

[1] Jer. 4: 2.   [2] Isa. 56: 1–2.   [3] Exod. 20: 8–10.   [4] Gen. 2: 1–3.

is within thy gates; that thy manservant and thy maidservant may rest as well as thou.

And thou shalt remember that thou wast a servant in the land of Egypt, and the Lord thy God brought thee out thence by a mighty hand and by a stretched out arm: therefore the Lord thy God commanded thee to keep the sabbath day.[1]

Also I gave them my sabbaths, to be a sign between me and them, that they might know that I am the Lord that sanctify them.[2]

Wherefore the children of Israel shall keep the sabbath, to observe the sabbath throughout their generations, for a perpetual covenant.

It is a sign between me and the children of Israel for ever: for in six days the Lord made heaven and earth, and on the seventh day he rested, and was refreshed.[3]

Six days thou shalt do thy work, and on the seventh day thou shalt rest: that thine ox and thine ass may have rest, and the son of thy handmaid, and the stranger, may be refreshed.[4]

And six years thou shalt sow thy land, and shalt gather in the increase thereof: but the seventh year thou shalt let it rest and lie fallow; that the poor of thy people may eat.[5]

And thou shalt number seven sabbaths of years unto thee, seven times seven years; and there shall be unto thee the days of seven sabbaths of years, even forty and

---

[1] Deut. 5: 12–15.
[2] Ezek. 20: 12.
[3] Exod. 31: 16–17.
[4] Exod. 23: 12.
[5] Exod. 23: 10.

nine years. Then shalt thou send abroad the loud trumpet on the tenth day of the seventh month; in the day of atonement shall ye send abroad the trumpet throughout all your land.

And ye shall hallow the fiftieth year, and proclaim liberty throughout the land unto all the inhabitants thereof: it shall be a jubile unto you; and ye shall return every man unto his possession, and ye shall return every man unto his family.[1]

Hear this, O ye that would swallow up the needy, and cause the poor of the land to fail, saying, When will the new moon be gone, that we may sell corn? and the sabbath, that we may set forth wheat? naking the ephah small, and the shekel great, and dealing falsely with balances of deceit; that we may buy the poor for silver, and the needy for a pair of shoes, and sell the refuse of the wheat.

The Lord hath sworn by the excellency of Jacob, Surely I will never forget any of their works.[2]

Thou [shalt] turn away thy foot from the sabbath, from doing thy pleasure on my holy day; and call the sabbath a delight, and the holy of the Lord honourable: and shalt honour it, not doing thine own ways, nor finding thine own pleasure, nor speaking thine own words.[3]

Also the strangers, that join themselves to the Lord, to minister unto him, and to love the name of the Lord, to be his servants, every one that keepeth the sabbath from profaning it, and holdeth fast by my covenant; them too will I bring to my holy mountain and make them joyful in my house of prayer.[4]

[1] Lev. 25: 8–10.   [2] Amos 8: 4–7.   [3] Isa. 58: 13 (A).   [4] Isa. 56: 6–7.

And it shall come to pass, that from one new moon to another, and from one sabbath to another, shall all flesh come to worship before me, saith the Lord.[1]

It is a sabbath unto the Lord.[2]

Ye shall be holy: for I the Lord your God am holy. Ye shall fear every man his mother, and his father, and ye shall keep my sabbaths: I am the Lord your God.[3]

HONOUR THY FATHER AND THY MOTHER.[4]

Then Judah came near unto him, and said, Oh my lord, let thy servant, I pray thee, speak a word in my lord's ears, and let not thine anger burn against thy servant: for thou art even as Pharaoh.

My lord asked his servants, saying, Have ye a father, or a brother? And we said unto my lord, We have a father, an old man, and a child of his old age, a little one; and his brother is dead, and he alone is left of his mother, and his father loveth him. And thou saidst unto thy servants, Bring him down unto me, that I may set mine eyes upon him. And we said unto my lord, The lad cannot leave his father: for if he should leave his father, his father would die. And thou saidst unto thy servants, Except your youngest brother come down with you, ye shall see my face no more.

And it came to pass when we came up unto thy servant my father, we told him the words of my lord. And our father said, Go again, buy us a little food. And we said, we cannot go down: if our youngest brother be with us, then will we go down: for we may not see the man's face, except our youngest brother be with us.

[1]Isa. 66: 23.   [2]Lev. 23: 3.   [3]Lev. 19: 2–3.   [4]Exod. 20: 12.

And thy servant my father said unto us, Ye know that my wife bare me two sons; and the one went out from me, and I said, Surely he is torn in pieces; and I have not seen him since; and if ye take this one also from me, and mischief befall him, ye shall bring down my gray hairs with sorrow to the grave.

Now therefore when I come to thy servant my father, and the lad be not with us; seeing that his life is bound up in the lad's life; it shall come to pass, when he seeth that the lad is not with us, that he will die: and thy servants shall bring down the gray hairs of thy servant our father with sorrow to the grave. For thy servant became surety for the lad unto my father, saying, If I bring him not unto thee, then shall I bear the blame to my father for ever.

Now therefore, let thy servant, I pray thee, abide instead of the lad a bondman to my lord; and let the lad go up with his brethren. For how shall I go up to my father, and the lad be not with me? lest I see the evil that shall come on my father.[1]

And Joseph said unto his brethren, I am Joseph; doth my father yet live? . . . Haste ye, and go up to my father, and say unto him, Thus saith thy son Joseph, God hath made me lord of all Egypt: come down unto me, tarry not: and thou shalt dwell in the land of Goshen, and thou shalt be near unto me, thou, and thy children, and thy children's children, and thy flocks, and thy herds, and all that thou hast: and there will I nourish thee.[2]

Children's children are the crown of old men;
And the glory of children are their fathers.[3]

[1] Gen. 44: 18-34.   [2] Gen. 45: 3, 9-11.   [3] Prov. 17: 6.

And it came to pass after these things, that one said to Joseph, Behold, thy father is sick: and he took with him his two sons, Manasseh and Ephraim. And one told Jacob, and said, Behold, thy son Joseph cometh unto thee: and Israel strengthened himself, and sat upon the bed.

And Jacob said unto Joseph, God Almighty appeared unto me at Luz in the land of Canaan, and blessed me, and said unto me, Behold, I will make thee fruitful, and multiply thee, and I will make of thee a company of peoples; and will give this land to thy seed after thee for an everlasting possession. And now thy two sons, which were born unto thee in the land of Egypt before I came unto thee into Egypt, are mine; Ephraim and Manasseh, even as Reuben and Simeon, shall be mine. And thy issue, which thou begettest after them, shall be thine; they shall be called after the name of their brethren in their inheritance.

And as for me, when I came from Paddan, Rachel died by me in the land of Canaan in the way, when there was still some way to come unto Ephrath: and I buried her there in the way to Ephrath (the same is Beth-lehem).

And Israel beheld Joseph's sons, and said, Who are these? And Joseph said unto his father, They are my sons, whom God hath given me here. And he said, Bring them, I pray thee, unto me, and I will bless them.[1]

The eye that mocketh at his father,
And despiseth to obey his mother,
The ravens of the valley shall pick it out,
And the young eagles shall eat it.[2]

[1] Prov. 30: 17.   [2] Gen. 48: 1–9.

Hearken to me, ye that follow after righteousness, ye that seek the Lord: look unto the rock whence ye were hewn, and to the hole of the pit whence ye were digged.

Look unto Abraham your father, and unto Sarah that bare you.[1]

For thou art our father, though Abraham knoweth us not, and Israel doth not acknowledge us: thou, O Lord, art our father; our redeemer from everlasting is thy name.[2]

A son honoureth his father, and a servant his master: if then I be a father, where is mine honour? and if I be a master, where is my fear? saith the Lord of hosts.[3]

But now, O Lord, thou art our father; we are the clay, and thou our potter; and we are all the work of thy hand. Be not wroth very sore, O Lord, neither remember iniquity for ever: behold, look, we beseech thee, we are all thy people.[4]

Have we not all one father? hath not one God created us? why do we deal treacherously every man against his brother?[5]

Thine own Friend, and thy father's Friend, forsake not.[6]

And despise not thy mother when she is old.[7]

Behold, I will send you Elijah the prophet before the great and terrible day of the Lord come. And he shall

[1] Isa. 51: 1–2.
[2] Isa. 63: 16.
[3] Mal. 1: 6.
[4] Isa. 64: 8–9.
[5] Mal. 2: 10.
[6] Prov. 27: 10—an old interpretation.
[7] Prov. 23: 22.

turn the heart of the fathers to their children, and the heart of the children to their fathers.[1]

Blessed is every one that feareth the Lord,
That walketh in his ways.
For thou shalt eat the labour of thy hands:
Happy shalt thou be, and it shall be well with thee.
   Thy wife shall be as a fruitful vine, in the innermost
      parts of thine house:
Thy children like olive plants, round about thy table.
Behold, that thus shall the man be blessed
That feareth the Lord.
   The Lord shall bless thee out of Zion:
And thou shalt see the good of Jerusalem all the days
      of thy life.
Yea, thou shalt see thy children's children.
Peace be upon Israel.[2]

Woe is me! for I am as when they have gathered the summer fruits, as the grape gleanings of the vintage; there is no cluster to eat; my soul desireth the first-ripe fig.

The godly man is perished out of the earth, and there is none upright among men: they all lie in wait for blood; they hunt every man his brother with a net. Their hands are upon that which is evil to do it diligently; the prince asketh, and the judge is ready for a reward; and the great man, he uttereth the mischief of his soul: thus they weave it together. The best of them is as a brier: the most upright is worse than a thorn hedge; the day of thy watchmen, even thy visitation, is come; now shall be their perplexity.

Trust ye not in a friend, put ye not confidence in a guide; keep the doors of thy mouth from her that lieth

---

[1]Mal. 4: 5–6.   [2]Ps. 128.

in thy bosom. For the son dishonoureth the father, the daughter riseth up against her mother, the daughter in law against her mother in law; a man's enemies are the men of his own house.[1]

Oh that I had in the wilderness a lodging place of wayfaring men; that I might leave my people, and go from them! for they be all adulterers, an assembly of treacherous men. And they bend their tongue as it were their bow for falsehood; and they are grown strong in the land, but not for truth: for they proceed from evil to evil, and they know not me, saith the Lord.

Take ye heed every one of his neighbour, and trust ye not in any brother; for every brother will utterly supplant, and every neighbour will go about with slanders. And they will deceive every one his neighbour, and will not speak the truth; they have taught their tongue to speak lies; they weary themselves to commit iniquity. Thine habitation is in the midst of deceit.[2]

Hear the word of the Lord, ye children of Israel: for the Lord hath a controversy with the inhabitants of the land, because there is no truth, nor mercy, nor knowledge of God in the land. There is nought but swearing and breaking faith, and killing, and stealing, and committing adultery; they break out, and blood toucheth blood.[3]

Will ye steal, murder, and commit adultery, and swear falsely, and burn incense unto Baal, and walk after other gods whom ye have not known, and come and stand before me in this house, which is called by my name, and say, We are delivered; that ye may do all these abominations?

---

[1] Mic. 7: 1–6.   [2] Jer. 9: 2–6.   [3] Hos. 4: 1–2.

Is this house, which is called by my name, become a den of robbers in your eyes?[1]

THOU SHALT DO NO MURDER.
 THOU SHALT NOT COMMIT ADULTERY.
 THOU SHALT NOT STEAL.
 THOU SHALT NOT BEAR FALSE WITNESS AGAINST THY NEIGHBOUR.
 THOU SHALT NOT COVET THY NEIGHBOUR'S HOUSE, THOU SHALT NOT COVET THY NEIGHBOUR'S WIFE, NOR HIS MANSERVANT, NOR HIS MAIDSERVANT, NOR HIS OX, NOR HIS ASS, NOR ANY THING THAT IS THY NIGHBOUR'S.[2]

And Cain told Abel his brother. And it came to pass, when they were in the field, that Cain rose up against Abel his brother, and slew him.[3]

These are of them that rebel against the light;
They know not the ways thereof,
Nor abide in the paths thereof.
The murderer riseth with the light, he killeth the poor
  and needy;
And in the night he is as a thief.
The eye also of the adulterer waiteth for the twilight,
Saying, No eye shall see me;
And he disguiseth his face.
In the dark they dig through houses:
They shut themselves up in the day-time;
They know not the light.[4]

Say unto wisdom, Thou art my sister;
And call understanding thy kinswoman:
That they may keep thee from the strange woman,
From the stranger which flattereth with her words.

[1] 7: 9–11. [2] Exod. 20: 13–17. [3] Gen. 4: 8. [4] Job. 24: 13–16.

   For at the window of my house
I looked forth through my lattice;
And I beheld among the simple ones,
I discerned among the youths,
A young man void of understanding,
Passing through the street near her corner,
And he went the way to her house;
In the twilight, in the evening of the day,
In the blackness of night and the darkness.
   And, behold, there met him a woman
With the attire of an harlot, and wily of heart.
She is clamorous and wilful;
Her feet abide not in her house;
Now she is in the streets, now in the broad places,
And lieth in wait at every corner.
So she caught him, and kissed him,
And with an impudent face she said unto him:
Sacrifices of peace offerings are with me;
This day have I paid my vows.
Therefore came I forth to meet thee,
Diligently to seek thy face, and I have found thee.
I have spread my couch with carpets of tapestry,
With striped cloths of the yarn of Egypt.
I have perfumed my bed
With myrrh, aloes, and cinnamon.
Come, let us take our fill of love until the morning;
Let us solace ourselves with loves.
For the goodman is not at home,
He is gone a long journey:
He hath taken a bag of money with him;
He will come home at the full moon.
   With her much fair speech she causeth him to yield,
With the flattering of her lips she forceth him away.
He goeth after her straightway,
As an ox goeth to the slaughter,

Or as fetters to the correction of the fool;
Till an arrow strike through his liver;
As a bird hasteth to the snare,
And knoweth not that it is for his life.
   Now, therefore, my sons, hearken unto me,
And attend to the words of my mouth.
Let not thine heart decline to her ways,
Go not astray in her paths.
For she hath cast down many wounded:
Yea, all her slain are a mighty host.
Her house is the way to Sheol,
Going down to the chambers of death.[1]

And it came to pass, at the return of the year, at the time when kings go out to battle, that David sent Joab, and his servants with him, and all Israel; and they destroyed the children of Ammon, and besieged Rabbah. But David tarried at Jerusalem.

And it came to pass at eventide, that David arose from off his bed, and walked upon the roof of the king's house: and from the roof he saw a woman bathing; and the woman was very beautiful to look upon. And David sent and inquired after the woman. And one said, Is not this Bathsheba, the daughter of Eliam, the wife of Uriah the Hittite?

And David sent messengers, and took her; and she came in unto him, and he lay with her; (for she was purified from her uncleanness;) and she returned unto her house. And the woman conceived; and she sent and told David, and said, I am with child.

And David sent to Joab, saying, Send me Uriah the Hittite. And Joab sent Uriah to David. And when Uriah was come unto him, David asked of him how Joab did, and how the people fared, and how the war

---
[1] Prov. 7: 4–27.

prospered. And David said to Uriah, Go down to thy house, and wash thy feet. And Uriah departed out of the king's house, and there followed him a mess of meat from the king. But Uriah slept at the door of the king's house with all the servants of his lord, and went not down to his house.

And when they had told David, saying, Uriah went not down unto his house, David said unto Uriah, Art thou not come from a journey? wherefore didst thou not go down unto thine house? And Uriah said unto David, The ark, and Israel, and Judah, abide in booths; and my lord Joab, and the servants of my lord, are encamped in the open field; shall I then go into mine house, to eat and to drink, and to lie with my wife? as thou livest, and as thy soul liveth, I will not do this thing.

And David said to Uriah, Tarry here to-day also, and to-morrow I will let thee depart. So Uriah abode in Jerusalem that day, and the morrow. And when David had called him, he did eat and drink before him; and he made him drunk: and at even he went out to lie on his bed with the servants of his lord, but to his house he went not down.

And it came to pass in the morning, that David wrote a letter to Joab, and sent it by the hand of Uriah. And he wrote in the letter, saying, Set ye Uriah in the forefront of the hottest battle, and retire ye from him, that he may be smitten, and die.

And it came to pass, when Joab kept watch upon the city, that he assigned Uriah unto the place where he knew that valiant men were. And the men of the city went out, and fought with Joab: and there fell some of the people, even of the servants of David; and Uriah the Hittite died also.

Then Joab sent and told David all the things concerning the war; and he charged the messenger, saying, When thou hast made an end of telling all the things concerning the war unto the king, it shall be that, if the king's wrath arise, and he say unto thee, Wherefore went ye so nigh unto the city to fight? knew ye not that they would shoot from the wall? who smote Abimelech the son of Jerubbesheth? did not a woman cast an upper millstone upon him from the wall, that he died at Thebez? why went ye so nigh the wall? then shalt thou say, Thy servant Uriah the Hittite is dead also.

So the messenger went, and came and shewed David all that Joab had sent him for. And the messenger said unto David, The men prevailed against us, and came out unto us into the field, and we were upon them even unto the entering of the gate. And the shooters shot at thy servants from off the wall; and some of the king's servants be dead, and thy servant Uriah the Hittite is dead also.

Then David said unto the messenger, Thus shalt thou say unto Joab, Let not this thing displease thee, for the sword devoureth one as well as another: make thy battle more strong against the city, and overthrow it: and encourage thou him.

And when the wife of Uriah heard that Uriah her husband was dead, she made lamentation for her husband. And when the mourning was past, David sent and took her home to his house, and she became his wife, and bare him a son.

But the thing that David had done displeased the Lord.

And the Lord sent Nathan unto David. And he came unto him, and said unto him, There were two men in one city; the one rich, and the other poor. The rich man had exceeding many flocks and herds; but the poor man had nothing, save one little ewe lamb, which he had bought and nourished up; and it grew up together with him, and with his children; it did eat of his own morsel, and drank of his own cup, and lay in his bosom, and was unto him as a daughter. And there came a traveller unto the rich man, and he spared to take of his own flock and of his own herd, to dress for the wayfaring man that was come unto him, but took the poor man's lamb, and dressed it for the man that was come to him.

And David's anger was greatly kindled against the man; and he said to Nathan, As the Lord liveth, the man that hath done this is worthy to die: and he shall restore the lamb fourfold, because he did this thing, and because he had no pity.

And Nathan said to David, Thou art the man.[1]

Can a man take fire in his bosom,
And his clothes not be burned?
Or can one walk upon hot coals,
And his feet not be scorched?
So he that goeth in to his neighbour's wife;
Whosoever toucheth her shall not be unpunished.[2]

And it came to pass after these things, that Naboth the Jezreelite had a vineyard, which was in Jezreel, hard by the palace of Ahab king of Samaria.

And Ahab spake unto Naboth, saying, Give me thy vineyard, that I may have it for a garden of herbs, because it is near unto my house; and I will give thee for it a better vineyard than it: or, if it seem good to thee, I will give thee the worth of it in money. And Naboth said to Ahab, The Lord forbid it me, that I should give the inheritance of my fathers unto thee. And Ahab came into his house heavy and displeased

[1] 2 Sam. 11: 1–12: 7. [2] Prov. 6: 27–29.

because of the word which Naboth the Jezreelite had spoken to him: for he had said, I will not give thee the inheritance of my fathers. And he laid him down upon his bed, and turned away his face, and would eat no bread.

But Jezebel his wife came to him, and said unto him, Why is thy spirit so sad, that thou eatest no bread? And he said unto her, Because I spake unto Naboth the Jezreelite, and said unto him, Give me thy vineyard for money; or else, if it please thee, I will give thee another vineyard for it: and he answered, I will not give thee my vineyard.

And Jebezel his wife said unto him, Dost thou now govern the kingdom of Israel? arise, and eat bread, and let thine heart be merry: I will give thee the vineyard of Naboth the Jezreelite. So she wrote letters in Ahab's name, and sealed them with his seal, and sent the letters unto the elders and to the nobles that were in his city, and that dwelt with Naboth. And she wrote in the letters, saying, Proclaim a fast, and set Naboth on high among the people: and set two men, sons of Belial, before him, and let them bear witness against him, saying, Thou didst curse God and the king. And then carry him out, and stone him, that he die.

And the men of his city, even the elders and the nobles who dwelt in his city, did as Jezebel had sent unto them, according as it was written in the letters which she had sent unto them. They proclaimed a fast, and set Naboth on high among the people. And the two men, sons of Belial, came in and sat before him: and the men of Belial bare witness against him, even against Naboth, in the presence of the people, saying, Naboth did curse God and the king. Then they carried him forth out of the city, and stoned him with stones, that he died.

Then they sent to Jezebel, saying, Naboth is stoned, and is dead. And it came to pass, when Jezebel heard that Naboth was stoned, and was dead, that Jezebel said to Ahab, Arise, take possession of the vineyard of Naboth the Jezreelite, which he refused to give thee for money: for Naboth is not alive, but dead. And it came to pass, when Ahab heard that Naboth was dead, that Ahab rose up to go down to the vineyard of Naboth the Jezreelite, to take possession of it.

And the word of the Lord came to Elijah the Tishbite, saying, Arise, go down to meet Ahab king of Israel, which dwelleth in Samaria: behold, he is in the vineyard of Naboth, whither he is gone down to take possession of it. And thou shalt speak unto him, saying, Thus saith the Lord, Hast thou killed, and also taken possession?

And thou shalt speak unto him saying, Thus saith the Lord, In the place where dogs licked the blood of Naboth shall dogs lick thy blood, even thine.[1]

My son, if sinners entice thee,
Consent thou not.
  If they say, Come with us,
Let us lay wait for blood,
Let us lurk privily for the innocent without cause;
Let us swallow them up alive as Sheol,
And whole, as those that go down into the pit;
We shall find all precious substance,
We shall fill our houses with spoil;
Thou shalt cast thy lot among us;
We will all have one purse:
  My son, walk not thou in the way with them;
Refrain thy foot from their path:
For their feet run to evil,
And they make haste to shed blood.

[1] 1 Kings 21: 1-19.

For in vain is the net spread,
In the eyes of any bird:
And these lay wait for their own blood,
They lurk privily for their own lives.
   So are the ways of every one that is greedy of gain;
It taketh away the life of the owners thereof.[1]

---

[1] Prov. 1: 10–19.

NINE

EVERYONE ACCORDING TO HIS WAYS[1]

> If thou doest well, shalt thou not be accepted?
> and if thou doest not well, sin coucheth at the
> door: and unto thee is its desire, but thou
> shouldest rule over it.[2]

The Biblical outlook with its strong sense of personal religion involves personal responsibility for actions performed; and personal responsibility, which is also responsibility to a person, leads in its turn to the conception of forgiveness and the saving value of contrition.

A tribal sense of communal sin is often praised nowadays but in practice it means the condoning of anonymous public cruelty. Communities, like committees, have no conscience.

Joseph, being seventeen years old, was feeding the flock with his brethren; and he was a lad with the sons of Bilhah, and with the sons of Zilpah, his father's wives: and Joseph brought the evil report of them unto their father.

Now Israel loved Joseph more than all his children, because he was the son of his old age: and he made him a coat of many colours. And his brethren saw that their father loved him more than all his brethren; and they hated him, and could not speak peaceably unto him.

And Joseph dreamed a dream, and he told it to his brethren: and they hated him yet the more. . . .

And his brethren went to feed their father's flock in

---
[1]Ezek. 18: 30.   [2]Gen. 4: 7 (m).

Shechem. And Israel said unto Joseph, Do not thy brethren feed the flock in Shechem? come, and I will send thee unto them. And he said to him, Here am I. And he said unto him, Go now, see whether it be well with thy brethren, and well with the flock; and bring me word again. So he sent him out of the vale of Hebron, and he came to Shechem. And a certain man found him, and, behold, he was wandering in the field: and the man asked him, saying, What seekest thou? And he said, I seek my brethren: tell me, I pray thee, where they are feeding the flock. And the man said, They are departed hence: for I heard them say, Let us go to Dothan. And Joseph went after his brethren, and found them in Dothan.

And they saw him afar off, and before he came near unto them, they conspired against him to slay him. And they said one to another, Behold, this dreamer cometh. Come now therefore, and let us slay him, and cast him into one of the pits, and we will say, An evil beast hath devoured him: and we shall see what will become of his dreams.

And Reuben heard it, and delivered him out of their hand; and said, Let us not take his life. And Reuben said unto them, Shed no blood; cast him into this pit that is in the wilderness, but lay no hand upon him: that he might deliver him out of their hand, to restore him to his father.

And it came to pass, when Joseph was come unto his brethren, that they stript Joseph of his coat, the coat of many colours that was on him; and they took him, and cast him into the pit. . . .

And Joseph was the governor over the land; he it was that sold to all the people of the land: and Joseph's brethren came, and bowed down themselves to him with their faces to the earth. And Joseph saw his brethren, and he knew them, but made himself strange unto them, and spake roughly with them; and he said unto them, Whence come ye? And they said, From the land of Canaan to buy food. And Joseph knew his brethren, but they knew not him.

And Joseph remembered the dreams which he dreamed of them, and said unto them, Ye are spies; to see the nakedness of the land ye are come. . . . If ye be true men, let one of your brethren be bound in your prison house: but go ye, carry corn for the famine of your houses; and bring your youngest brother unto me; so shall your words be verified, and ye shall not die. And they did so.

And they said one to another, We are verily guilty concerning our brother, in that we saw the distress of his soul, when he besought us, and we would not hear; therefore is this distress come upon us.

And Reuben answered them, saying, Spake I not unto you, saying, Do not sin against the child; and ye would not hear? therefore also, behold, his blood is required.[1]

And surely your blood, the blood of your lives, will I require; at the hand of every beast will I require it: and at the hand of man, even at the hand of every man's brother, will I require the life of man.

Whoso sheddeth man's blood, by man shall his blood be shed: for in the image of God made he man.[2]

He that smiteth a man, so that he die, shall surely be put to death.

And if a man lie not in wait, but God deliver him into his hand; then will I appoint thee a place whither he shall flee.

[1] Gen. 37: 2–5, 12–24; 42: 6–9, 19–22. [2] Gen. 9: 5–6.

And if a man come presumptuously upon his neighbour, to slay him with guile; thou shalt take him from mine altar, that he may die.[1]

And he that smiteth any man mortally shall surely be put to death; and he that smiteth a beast mortally shall make it good: life for life.[2]

Woe unto them that join house to house, that lay field to field, till there be no room, and ye be made to dwell alone in the midst of the land! In mine ears saith the Lord of hosts, Of a truth many houses shall be desolate, even great and fair, without inhabitant.[3]

Let them be before the Lord continually,
That he may cut off the memory of them from the earth.
Because that he [they] remembered not to show mercy,
But persecuted the poor and needy man,
And the broken in heart, to slay them.[4]

For he hath brought down them that dwell on high, the lofty city; he layeth it low, he layeth it low even to the ground; he bringeth it even to the dust.
The foot shall tread it down; even the feet of the poor, and the steps of the needy.[5]

Because thou hast spoiled many nations, all the remnant of the peoples shall spoil thee; because of men's blood, and for the violence done to the land, to the city and to all that dwell therein.[6]

The violence done to Lebanon shall cover thee, and the destruction of the beasts, which made them afraid.[7]

[1]Exod. 21: 12–14. [3]Isa. 5: 8–9. [5]Isa. 26: 5–6. [7]Hab. 2: 17.
[2]Lev. 24: 17–18. [4]Ps. 109: 15–16. [6]Hab. 2: 8.

O God, the God of the spirits of all flesh, shall one man sin, and wilt thou be wroth with all the congregation?[1]

Lo, I have sinned, and I have done perversely: but these sheep, what have they done?[2]

Thou seekest to destroy a city and a mother in Israel: why wilt thou swallow up the inheritance of the Lord?
And Joab answered and said, Far be it, far be it from me, that I should swallow up or destroy. The matter is not so: but a man of the hill country of Ephraim, Sheba the son of Bichri by name, hath lifted up his hand against the king, even against David: deliver him only, and I will depart from the city.
And the woman said unto Joab, Behold, his head shall be thrown to thee over the wall. Then the woman went unto all the people in her wisdom. And they cut off the head of Sheba the son of Bichri, and threw it out to Joab. And he blew the trumpet, and they were dispersed from the city, every man to his tent.[3]

And it came to pass on the morrow, that Moses said unto the people, Ye have sinned a great sin: and now I will go up unto the Lord; peradventure I shall make atonement for your sin.
And Moses returned unto the Lord, and said, Oh, this people have sinned a great sin, and have made gods of gold. Yet now, if thou wilt forgive their sin—; and if not, blot me, I pray thee, out of thy book which thou hast written.
And the Lord said unto Moses, Whosoever hath sinned against me, him will I blot out of my book.[4]

[1]Num. 16: 22.   [2]2 Sam. 24: 17.   [3]2 Sam. 20: 19–22.   [4]Exod. 32: 30–33.

Son of man, when a land sinneth against me by committing a trespass, and I stretch out mine hand upon it, and break the staff of the bread thereof, and send famine upon it, and cut off from it man and beast; though these three men, Noah, Daniel, and Job, were in it, they should deliver but their own souls by their righteousness, saith the Lord God.

If I cause noisome beasts to pass through the land, and they spoil it, so that it be desolate, that no man may pass through because of the beasts; though these three men were in it, as I live, saith the Lord God, they shall deliver neither sons nor daughters; they only shall be delivered, but the land shall be desolate.

Or if I bring a sword upon that land, and say, Sword, go through the land; so that I cut off from it man and beast; though these three men were in it, as I live, saith the Lord God, they shall deliver neither sons nor daughters, but they only shall be delivered themselves.

Or if I send a pestilence into that land, and pour out my fury upon it in blood, to cut off from it man and beast: though Noah, Daniel, and Job, were in it, as I live, saith the Lord God, they shall deliver neither son nor daughter; they shall but deliver their own souls by their righteousness.[1]

What mean ye, that ye use this proverb concerning the land of Israel, saying, The fathers have eaten sour grapes, and the children's teeth are set on edge? As I live, saith the Lord God, ye shall not have occasion any more to use this proverb in Israel.

Behold, all souls are mine; as the soul of the father, so also the soul of the son is mine: the soul that sinneth, it shall die.[2]

[1] Ezek. 14: 13-20.   [2] Ezek. 18: 2-4.

The fathers shall not be put to death for the children, neither shall the children be put to death for the fathers: every man shall be put to death for his own sin.[1]

In those days they shall say no more, The fathers have eaten sour grapes, and the children's teeth are set on edge. But every one shall die for his own iniquity: every man that eateth the sour grapes, his teeth shall be set on edge.[2]

And thou, son of man, say unto the house of Israel: Thus ye speak, saying, Our transgressions and our sins are upon us, and we pine away in them; how then should we live? Say unto them, As I live, saith the Lord God, I have no pleasure in the death of the wicked; but that the wicked turn from his way and live: turn ye, turn ye from your evil ways; for why will ye die, O house of Israel?

And thou, son of man, say unto the children of thy people, The righteousness of the righteous shall not deliver him in the day of his transgression; and as for the wickedness of the wicked, he shall not fall thereby in the day that he turneth from his wickedness: neither shall he that is righteous be able to live thereby in the day that he sinneth.

When I say to the righteous, that he shall surely live; if he trust to his righteousness, and commit iniquity, none of his righteous deeds shall be remembered; but in his iniquity that he hath committed, therein shall he die. Again, when I say unto the wicked, Thou shalt surely die; if he turn from his sin, and do that which is lawful and right; if the wicked restore the pledge, give again that he had taken by robbery, walk in the statutes of life, committing no iniquity; he shall surely live, he shall not die.

[1] Deut. 24. 16.   [2] Jer. 31: 29–30.

None of his sins that he hath committed shall be remembered against him: he hath done that which is lawful and right; he shall surely live.[1]

Therefore I will judge you, O house of Israel, every one according to his ways, saith the Lord God.
Return ye, and turn yourselves from all your transgressions; so iniquity shall not be your ruin. Cast away from you all your transgressions, wherein ye have transgressed; and make you a new heart and a new spirit: for why will ye die, O house of Israel?
For I have no pleasure in the death of him that dieth, saith the Lord God: wherefore turn yourselves, and live.[2]

If one man sin against another, God shall judge him: but if a man sin against the Lord, who shall intreat for him?[3]

Before the Lord shall ye be clean.[4]

The Lord is nigh unto them that are of a broken heart,
And saveth such as be of a contrite spirit.[5]

Have mercy upon me, O God, according to thy lovingkindness:
According to the multitude of thy tender mercies blot out my transgressions.
Wash me thoroughly from mine iniquity,
And cleanse me from my sin.
For I acknowledge my transgressions:
And my sin is ever before me.
Against thee, thee only, have I sinned,
And done that which is evil in thy sight:

---

[1] Ezek. 33: 10–16. [3] 1 Sam. 2: 25. [5] Ps. 34: 18.
[2] Ezek. 18: 30–32. [4] Lev. 16: 30 (OA).

That thou mayest be justified when thou speakest,
And be clear when thou judgest.
 Behold, I was shapen in iniquity;
And in sin did my mother conceive me.
Behold, thou desirest truth in the inward parts:
And in the hidden part thou shalt make me to know wisdom.
Purge me with hyssop, and I shall be clean:
Wash me, and I shall be whiter than snow.
Make me to hear joy and gladness;
That the bones which thou hast broken may rejoice.
Hide thy face from my sins,
And blot out all mine iniquities.
 Create in me a clean heart, O God,
And renew a right spirit within me.
Cast me not away from thy presence;
And take not thy holy spirit from me.
Restore unto me the joy of thy salvation:
And uphold me with a free spirit.
 Then will I teach transgressors thy ways;
And sinners shall be converted unto thee.
Deliver me from bloodguiltiness, O God, thou God of my salvation;
And my tongue shall sing aloud of thy righteousness.
 O Lord, open thou my lips;
And my mouth shall shew forth thy praise.
For thou delightest not in sacrifice; else would I give it:
Thou hast no pleasure in burnt offering.
The sacrifices of God are a broken spirit:
A broken and a contrite heart, O God, thou wilt not despise.[1]

My heart is ready, O God, my heart is ready.[2]

With the merciful thou wilt shew thyself merciful.[3]

[1] Ps. 51: 1–17. [2] Ps. 57: 7 (A). [3] 2 Sam. 22: 26.

TEN

MY PEOPLE, MY CHOSEN[1]

An holy people unto the Lord thy God.[2]

The 'chosen people'—but chosen for what? Not for pleasure, surely, nor for power. No religion is an acceptance of the present condition or a warrant for terrestial happiness. If happiness comes, it is incidental to the performance of function, or, in more solemn language, of mission; and the human situation, spiritual as well as material, is never so satisfactory that it should not, and can not, be bettered. The 'choice' of a people means the acceptance by them of a specific vocation; and in this case the nature of the vocation is indicated clearly from the first: it is to practice and exemplify a new way of living.

Men have always resented instruction, however indirect; and the greater their need of it, the greater is their resentment. The Servants of all peoples, in all ages, and in all countries, are brought invariably to contempt and suffering.

Adam, Seth, Enosh; Kenan, Mahalalel, Jared; Enoch, Methuselah, Lamech; Noah, Shem, Ham, and Japheth.
. . . Shem, Arpachshad, Shelah; Eber, Peleg, Reu; Serug, Nahor, Terah; Abram (the same is Abraham).[3]

Abraham thy friend.[4]

When he was but one I called him.[5]

[1] Isa. 43: 20.   [3] 1 Chron. 1: 1–4, 24–27.   [4] 2 Chron. 20: 7.
[2] Deut. 7: 6.   [5] Isa. 52: 2.

130

For I have known him, to the end that he may command his children and his household after him, that they may keep the way of the Lord, to do justice and judgement.[1]

And Abraham begat Isaac. The sons of Isaac; Esau, and Israel.[2]

Israel, whom I have chosen.[3]

Israel, my son, my firstborn.[4]

Israel was holiness unto the Lord, the firstfruits of his increase.[5]

For the Lord's portion is his people;
Jacob is the lot of his inheritance.
  He found him in a desert land,
And in the waste howling wilderness;
He compassed him about, he cared for him,
He kept him as the apple of his eye:
As an eagle that stirreth up her nest,
That fluttereth over her young,
He spread abroad his wings, he took them,
He bare them on his pinions:
  The Lord alone did lead him,
And there was no strange god with him.[6]

I bare you on eagles' wings, and brought you unto myself.
  Now therefore, if ye will obey my voice indeed, and keep my covenant, then ye shall be a peculiar treasure unto me from among all peoples: for all the earth is

[1] Gen. 18: 19.
[2] 1 Chron. 1: 34.
[3] Isa. 44: 1.
[4] Exod. 4: 22.
[5] Jer. 2: 3.
[6] Deut. 32: 9-12.

mine: and ye shall be unto me a kingdom of priests, and an holy nation.[1]

I will take you to me for a people, and I will be to you a God.[2]

The people which I formed for myself, that they might set forth my praise.[3]

Ye that know righteousness, the people in whose heart is my law.[4]

When Israel was a child, then I loved him, and called my son out of Egypt. As they called them, so they went from them: they sacrificed unto the Baalim, and burned incense to graven images.
   Yet I taught Ephraim to go; I took them on my arms; but they knew not that I healed them. I drew them with cords of a man, with bands of love.[5]

To love the Lord thy God with all thine heart, and with all thy soul, that thou mayest live.[6]

Hear, O Israel: the Lord our God, the Lord is one: and thou shalt love the Lord thy God with all thine heart, and with all thy soul, and with all thy might.
   And these words, which I command thee this day, shall be upon thine heart: and thou shalt teach them diligently unto thy children, and shalt talk of them when thou sittest in thine house, and when thou walkest by the way, and when thou liest down, and when thou risest up. And thou shalt bind them for a sign upon thine hand, and they shall be for frontlets between

---

[1] Exod. 19: 4–6. [3] Isa. 43: 21. [5] Hos. 11: 1–4.
[2] Exod. 6: 7. [4] Isa. 51: 7. [6] Deut. 30: 6.

thine eyes. And thou shalt write them upon the door posts of thy house, and upon thy gates.[1]

This day the Lord thy God commandeth thee to do these statutes and judgements: thou shalt therefore keep and do them with all thine heart, and with all thy soul.

Thou hast avouched the Lord this day to be thy God, and that thou shouldest walk in his ways, and keep his statutes, and his commandments, and his judgements, and hearken unto his voice.

And the Lord hath avouched thee this day to be a peculiar people unto himself, as he hath promised thee, and that thou shouldest keep all his commandments; and to make thee high above all nations which he hath made, in praise, and in name, and in honour; and that thou mayest be an holy people unto the Lord thy God, as he hath spoken.[2]

I call heaven and earth to witness against you this day, that I have set before thee life and death, the blessing and the curse: therefore choose life, that thou mayst live, thou and thy seed: to love the Lord thy God, to obey his voice, and to cleave unto him: for he is thy life, and the length of thy days.[3]

Ye stand this day all of you before the Lord your God; your heads, your tribes, your elders, and your officers, even all the men of Israel, your little ones, your wives, and thy stranger that is in the midst of thy camps, from the hewer of thy wood unto the drawer of thy water: that thou shouldest enter into the covenant of the Lord thy God, and into his oath, which the Lord thy God maketh with thee this day: that he may

[1] Deut. 6: 4–9 (M).   [2] Deut. 26: 16–19.   [3] Deut. 30: 19–20.

establish thee this day unto himself for a people, and that he may be unto thee a God, as he spake unto thee, and as he sware unto thy fathers, to Abraham, to Isaac, and to Jacob.

Neither with you only do I make this covenant and this oath; but with him that standeth here with us this day before the Lord our God, and also with him that is not here with us this day.[1]

And as for me, this is my covenant with them, saith the Lord: my spirit that is upon thee, and my words which I have put in thy mouth, shall not depart out of thy mouth, nor out of the mouth of thy seed, nor out of the mouth of thy seed's seed, saith the Lord, from henceforth and for ever.[2]

For he established a testimony in Jacob,
And appointed a law in Israel,
Which he commanded our fathers,
That they should make them known to their children:
That the generation to come might know them, even
    the children which should be born;
Who should arise and tell them to their children:
That they might set their hope in God,
And not forget the works of God,
But keep his commandments.[3]

This thing I commanded them, saying, Hearken unto my voice, and I will be your God, and ye shall be my people: and walk ye in all the way that I command you, that it may be well with you.

But they hearkened not, nor inclined their ear, but walked in their own counsels and in the stubbornness of their evil heart, and went backward and not forward.

[1]Deut. 29: 10-15. [2]Isa. 59: 21. [3]Ps. 78: 5-7

Since the day that your fathers came forth out of the land of Egypt unto this day, I have sent unto you all my servants the prophets, daily rising up early and sending them: yet they hearkened not unto me, nor inclined their ear, but made their neck stiff: they did worse than their fathers.[1]

Ye eat with the blood, and lift up your eyes unto your idols, and shed blood: and shall ye possess the land? Ye stand upon your sword, ye work abomination, and ye defile every one his neighbour's wife: and shall ye possess the land?[2]

Are ye not as the children of the Ethiopians unto me, O children of Israel? saith the Lord. Have not I brought up Israel out of the land of Egypt, and the Philistines from Caphtor, and the Syrians from Kir?[3]

Thus saith the Lord God unto Jerusalem: Thy birth and thy nativity is of the land of the Canaanite; the Amorite was thy father, and thy mother was an Hittite.[4]

And Joshua said unto all the people, Thus saith the Lord, the God of Israel, Your fathers dwelt of old time beyond the River, even Terah, the father of Abraham, and the father of Nahor; and they served other gods. And I took your father Abraham from beyond the River, and led him throughout all the land of Canaan, and multiplied his seed, and gave him Isaac. And I gave unto Isaac Jacob and Esau: and I gave unto Esau mount Seir, to possess it; and Jacob and his children went down into Egypt. . . . Now therefore fear the Lord, and serve him in sincerity and truth: and

[1] Jer. 7: 23-26.   [2] Ezek. 33: 25-26.   [3] Amos. 9: 7.   [4] Ezek. 16: 3.

put away the gods which your fathers served beyond the River, and in Egypt; and serve ye the Lord.

And if it seem evil unto you to serve the Lord, choose you this day whom ye will serve; whether the gods which your fathers served that were beyond the River, or the gods of the Amorites, in whose land ye dwell. . . . And Joshua said unto the people, Ye cannot serve the Lord; for he is an holy God; he is a jealous God; he will not forgive you your transgression nor your sins. If ye forsake the Lord, and serve strange gods, then he will turn and do you evil, and consume you, after that he hath done you good. And the people said unto Joshua, Nay; but we will serve the Lord.

And Joshua said unto the people, Ye are witnesses against yourselves that ye have chosen you the Lord, to serve him. And they said, We are witnesses.[1]

Ye are my witnesses, saith the Lord, and my servant whom I have chosen.[2]

Thou, Israel, my servant, Jacob whom I have chosen, the seed of Abraham, my friend; thou whom I have taken hold of from the ends of the earth, and called thee from the corners thereof, and said unto thee, Thou art my servant, I have chosen thee and not cast thee away.[3]

Behold my servant, whom I uphold; my chosen, in whom my soul delighteth: I have put my spirit upon him: he shall bring forth judgement to the Gentiles. He shall not cry, nor lift up, nor cause his voice to be heard in the street. A bruised reed shall he not break, and the smoking flax shall he not quench: he shall bring forth judgement in truth.

[1]Josh. 24: 2–4, 14–15, 19–22.　　[2]Isa. 43: 10.　　[3]Isa. 41: 8–9.

He shall not fail nor be discouraged, till he have set judgement in the earth; and the isles shall wait for his law.[1]

Listen, O isles, unto me; and hearken, ye peoples, from far: the Lord hath called me from the womb; from the bowels of my mother hath he made mention of my name: and he hath made my mouth like a sharp sword, in the shadow of his hand hath he hid me; and he hath made me a polished shaft, in his quiver hath he kept me close: and he said unto me, Thou art my servant; Israel, in whom I will be glorified. But I said, I have laboured in vain, I have spent my strength for nought and vanity: yet surely my judgement is with the Lord, and my recompence with my God.

And now saith the Lord that formed me from the womb to be his servant, to bring Jacob again to him, and that Israel be gathered unto him: (for I am honourable in the eyes of the Lord, and my God is become my strength:) yea, he saith, It is too light a thing that thou shouldest be my servant to raise up the tribes of Jacob, and to restore the preserved of Israel: I will also give thee for a light to the Gentiles, that thou mayest be my salvation unto the end of the earth.[2]

All the ends of the earth shall see the salvation of our God.[3]

Behold, my servant shall deal wisely, he shall be exalted and lifted up, and shall be very high. Like as many were astonied at thee, (his visage was so marred more than any man, and his form more than the sons of men,) so shall he sprinkle many nations; kings shall

[1] Isa. 42: 1–4.   [2] Isa. 49: 1–6.   [3] Isa. 52: 10.

shut their mouths at him: for that which had not been told them shall they see; and that which they had not heard shall they understand.

Who hath believed our report? and to whom hath the arm of the Lord been revealed? For he grew up before him as a tender plant, and as a root out of a dry ground: he hath no form nor comeliness; and when we see him, there is no beauty that we should desire him. He was despised, and rejected of men; a man of sorrows, and acquainted with grief: and as one from whom men hide their face he was despised, and we esteemed him not.

Surely he hath borne our griefs, and carried our sorrows: yet we did esteem him stricken, smitten of God, and afflicted. But he was wounded for our transgressions, he was bruised for our iniquities: the chastisement of our peace was upon him; and with his stripes we are healed. All we like sheep have gone astray; we have turned every one to his own way; and the Lord hath laid on him the iniquity of us all.

He was oppressed, yet he humbled himself and opened not his mouth; as a lamb that is led to the slaughter, and as a sheep that before her shearers is dumb; yea, he opened not his mouth. By oppression and judgement he was taken away; and as for his generation, who among them considered that he was cut off out of the land of the living? for the transgression of my people was he stricken. And they made his grave with the wicked, and with the rich in his death; although he had done no violence, neither was any deceit in his mouth.

Yet it pleased the Lord to bruise him; he hath put him to grief: when thou shalt make his soul an offering for sin, he shall see his seed, he shall prolong his days, and the pleasure of the Lord shall prosper in his hand.

He shall see the travail of his soul, and shall be satisfied: by his knowledge shall my righteous servant justify many: and he shall bear their iniquities. Therefore will I divide him a portion with the great, and he shall divide the spoil with the strong; because he poured out his soul unto death, and was numbered with the transgressors; yet he bare the sin of many, and made intercession for the transgressors.[1]

O thou afflicted, tossed with tempest, and not comforted.[2]

I, even I, am he that comforteth you.[3]

As one whom his mother comforteth, so will I comfort you.[4]

I remember for thee the kindness of thy youth, the love of thine espousals; how thou wentest after me in the wilderness.[5]

In his love and in his pity he redeemed them.[6]

Thus saith the Lord, the redeemer of Israel, and his Holy One, to him whom man despiseth, to whom the nation abhorreth, to a servant of rulers: Kings shall see and arise; princes, and they shall worship; because of the Lord that is faithful, even the Holy One of Israel, who hath chosen thee.[7]

He hath torn, and he will heal us; he hath smitten, and he will bind us up.[8]

[1]Isa. 52: 13–53: 12. [2]Isa. 51: 12. [3]Jer. 2: 2. [7]Isa. 49: 7.
[3]Isa. 54: 11. [4]Isa. 66: 13. [6]Isa. 63: 9. [8]Hos. 6: 1.

I have called thee by thy name, thou art mine. When thou passeth through the waters, I will be with thee; and through the rivers, they shall not overflow thee: when thou walkest through the fire, thou shalt not be burned; neither shall the flame kindle upon thee.[1]

Hear ye indeed, but understand not; and see ye indeed, but perceive not.[2]

Who is blind, but my servant? or deaf, as my messenger that I send? who is blind as he that is at peace with me, and blind as the Lord's servant? Thou seest many things, but thou observest not; his ears are open, but he heareth not. It pleased the Lord, for his righteousness' sake, to magnify the law, and make it honourable. But this is a people robbed and spoiled; they are all of them snared in holes.[3]

Remember these things, O Jacob; and Israel, for thou art my servant: I have formed thee; thou art my servant: O Israel, thou shalt not be forgotten of me.[4]

And that which cometh into your mind shall not be at all; in that ye say, We will be as the nations, as the families of the countries, to serve wood and stone. As I live, saith the Lord God, surely with a mighty hand, and with a stretched out arm, and with fury poured out, will I be king over you.[5]

I will be sanctified in them that come nigh me.[6]

Be ye clean, ye that bear the vessels of the Lord.[7]

---

[1]Isa. 43: 1–2. [2]Isa. 42: 19–22. [5]Ezek 20: 32–33. [7]Isa. 52: 11.
[3]Isa. 6: 9. [4]Isa. 44: 21. [6]Lev. 10: 3.

ELEVEN

THE GOD OF JUDGEMENT[1]

> For the Lord is a God of knowledge,
> And by him actions are weighed.[2]

A main point in the following Section is that the God of the Hebrew Bible is a God of universal justice. He respects neither persons nor peoples, and least of all his own.

It should be read in close conjunction with the preceding. The Jews of the Bible are the only 'chosen people' who, through the mouth of their prophets, have called for judgement on themselves. They have also, and in good measure, received it.

Woe unto you that desire the day of the Lord! wherefore would ye have the day of the Lord? it is darkness, and not light.

As if a man did flee from a lion, and a bear met him; or went into the house and leaned his hand on the wall, and a serpent bit him. Shall not the day of the Lord be darkness, and not light? even very dark, and no brightness in it?[3]

Ye have wearied the Lord with your words. Yet ye say, Wherein have we wearied him? In that ye say, Every one that doeth evil is good in the sight of the Lord, and he delighteth in them; or where is the God of judgement?

Behold, I send my messenger, and he shall prepare

[1]Mal. 2: 17.   [2]1 Sam. 2: 3.   [3]Amos 5: 18-20.

the way before me: and the Lord, whom ye seek, shall suddenly come to his temple; and the messenger of the covenant, whom ye delight in, behold, he cometh, saith the Lord of hosts. But who may abide the day of his coming? and who shall stand when he appeareth? for he is like a refiner's fire.[1]

The Lord will enter into judgement with the elders of his people, and the princes thereof: It is ye that have eaten up the vineyard; the spoil of the poor is in your houses.

What mean ye that ye crush my people, and grind the face of the poor? saith the Lord, the Lord of hosts.[2]

In thy skirts is found the blood of the souls of the innocent poor: I have not found it at the place of breaking in, but upon all these.

Yet thou saidst, I am innocent; surely his anger is turned away from me. Behold, I will enter into judgement with thee, because thou sayest, I have not sinned.[3]

Thus saith the Lord: For three transgressions of Judah, yea, for four, I will not turn away the punishment thereof; because they have rejected the law of the Lord, and have not kept his statutes, and their lies have caused them to err, after the which their fathers did walk: but I will send a fire upon Judah, and it shall devour the palaces of Jerusalem.

Thus saith the Lord: For three transgressions of Israel, yea, for four, I will not turn away the punishment thereof; because they have sold the righteous for silver, and the needy for a pair of shoes: that pant after the dust of the earth on the head of the poor, and turn aside the way of the meek: and a man and his father

---

[1] Mal. 2: 17–3: 2. [2] Isa. 3: 14–15. [3] Jer. 2: 34–35.

will go unto the same maid, to profane my holy name: and they lay themselves down beside every altar upon clothes taken in pledge, and in the house of their God they drink the wine of such as have been fined.[1]

Forget not the life of thy poor for ever.
Have respect unto the covenant:
For the dark places of the earth are full of the habitations of violence.
O let not the oppressed return ashamed:
Let the poor and needy praise thy name.
   Arise, O God, plead thine own cause.[2]

The Lord standeth up to plead, and standeth to judge the peoples.[3]

Thus saith the Lord: For three transgressions of Damascus, yea, for four, I will not turn away the punishment thereof; because they have threshed Gilead with threshing instruments of iron. . . .

  Thus saith the Lord: For three transgressions of Gaza, yea, for four, I will not turn away the punishment thereof; because they carried away captive the whole people, to deliver them up to Edom. . . .

  Thus saith the Lord: For three transgressions of Tyre, yea, for four, I will not turn away the punishment thereof; because they delivered up the whole people to Edom, and remembered not the brotherly covenant. . . .

  Thus saith the Lord: For three transgressions of Edom, yea, for four, I will not turn away the punishment thereof; because he did pursue his brother with the sword, and did cast off all pity, and his anger did tear perpetually, and he kept his wrath for ever. . . .

[1] Amos. 2: 4–8.   [2] Ps. 74: 19–22.   [3] Isa. 3: 13.

Thus saith the Lord: For three transgressions of the children of Ammon, yea, for four, I will not turn away the punishment thereof; because they have ripped up the women with child of Gilead, that they might enlarge their border.[1]

Then he cried in mine ears with a loud voice, saying, Cause ye them that have charge over the city to draw near, every man with his destroying weapon in his hand.

And behold, six men came from the way of the upper gate, which lieth toward the north, every man with his slaughter weapon in his hand; and one man in the midst of them clothed in linen, with a writer's inkhorn by his side. And they went in, and stood beside the brasen altar. And the glory of the God of Israel was gone up from the cherub, whereupon it was, to the threshold of the house: and he called to the man clothed in linen, which had the writer's inkhorn by his side. And the Lord said unto him, Go through the midst of the city, through the midst of Jerusalem, and set a mark upon the foreheads of the men that sigh and that cry for all the abominations that be done in the midst thereof.

And to the others he said in mine hearing, Go ye through the city after him, and smite: let not your eye spare, neither have ye pity: slay utterly the old man, the young man and the maiden, and little children and women; but come not near any man upon whom is the mark; and begin at my sanctuary.[2]

They rebelled, and grieved his holy spirit: therefore he was turned to be their enemy, and himself fought against them.[3]

[1] Amos 1: 3, 6, 9, 11, 13.   [2] Ezek. 9: 1–6.   [3] Isa. 63: 10.

You only have I known of all the families of the earth: therefore I will visit upon you all your iniquities.[1]

Thus saith the Lord God unto the land of Israel, An end: the end is come upon the four corners of the land. Now is the end upon thee, and I will send mine anger upon thee, and will judge thee according to thy ways; and I will bring upon thee all thine abominations. And mine eye shall not spare thee, neither will I have pity: but I will bring thy ways upon thee, and thine abominations shall be in the midst of thee: and ye shall know that I am the Lord.

Thus saith the Lord God: An evil, an only evil; behold, it cometh. An end is come, the end is come, it awaketh against thee; behold, it cometh. Thy doom is come unto thee, O inhabitant of the land; the time is come, the day is near; a day of tumult, and not of joyful shouting, upon the mountains.

Now will I shortly pour out my fury upon thee, and accomplish mine anger against thee, and will judge thee according to thy ways; and I will bring upon thee all thine abominations. And mine eye shall not spare, neither will I have pity: I will bring upon thee according to thy ways, and thine abominations shall be in the midst of thee; and ye shall know that I the Lord do smite.[2]

My people hath been lost sheep: their shepherds have caused them to go astray, they have turned them away on the mountains: they have gone from mountain to hill, they have forgotten their resting place. All that found them have devoured them: and their adversaries said, We offend not, because they have sinned against

---

[1] Amos. 3: 2. [2] Ezek. 7: 2-9.

the Lord, the habitation of justice, even the Lord, the hope of their fathers.

Flee out of the midst of Babylon, and go forth out of the land of the Chaldeans, and be as the he-goats before the flocks. For, lo, I will stir up and cause to come up against Babylon an assembly of great nations from the north country: and they shall set themselves in array against her; from thence she shall be taken.[1]

Israel is a scattered sheep; the lions have driven him away: first the king of Assyria hath devoured him: and last this Nebuchadnezzar king of Babylon hath broken his bones.

Therefore thus saith the Lord of hosts, the God of Israel: Behold, I will punish the king of Babylon and his land, as I have punished the king of Assyria.[2]

Hear ye the rod, and who hath appointed it.[3]

Ho Assyrian, the rod of mine anger, the staff in whose hand is mine indignation! I will send him against a profane nation, and against the people of my wrath will I give him a charge to take the spoil, and to take the prey, and to tread them down like the mire of the streets.

Howbeit he meaneth not so, neither doth his heart think so; but it is in his heart to destroy, and to cut off nations not a few. For he saith, Are not my princes all of them kings? Is not Calno as Carchemish? is not Hamath as Arpad? is not Samaria as Damascus? As my hand hath found the kingdoms of the idols, whose graven images did excel them of Jerusalem and of Samaria; shall I not, as I have done unto Samaria and her idols, so do to Jerusalem and her idols?

[1] Jer. 50: 6-9.   [2] Jer. 50: 17-18.   [3] Mic. 6: 9.

Wherefore it shall come to pass, that when the Lord hath performed his whole work upon mount Zion and on Jerusalem, I will punish the fruit of the stout heart of the king of Assyria, and the glory of his high looks. For he hath said, By the strength of my hand I have done it, and by my wisdom; for I am prudent: and I have removed the bounds of the peoples, and have robbed their treasures, and I have brought down as a valiant man them that sit on thrones: and my hand hath found as a nest the riches of the peoples; and as one gathereth eggs that are forsaken, have I gathered all the earth: and there was none that moved the wing, or that opened the mouth, or chirped.

Shall the axe boast itself against him that heweth therewith? shall the saw magnify itself against him that shaketh it? as if a rod should shake them that lift it up, or as if a staff should lift up him that is not wood.[1]

... he whose might is his god.

Art not thou from everlasting, O Lord my God, mine Holy One? we shall not die. O Lord, thou hast ordained him for judgement; and thou, O Rock, hast established him for correction. Thou that art of purer eyes than to behold evil, and that canst not look on perverseness, wherefore lookest thou upon them that deal treacherously, and holdest thy peace when the wicked swalloweth up the man that is more righteous than he; and makest men as the fishes of the sea, as the creeping things, that have no ruler over them? He taketh up all of them with the angle, he catcheth them in his net, and gathereth them in his drag: therefore he rejoiceth and is glad. Therefore he sacrificeth unto his net, and burneth incense unto his drag; because by them his portion is fat, and his meat plenteous.

[1] Isa. 10: 5–15.

Shall he therefore empty his net, and not spare to slay the nations continually?

I will stand upon my watch, and set me upon the tower, and will look forth to see what he will speak with me, and what I shall answer concerning my complaint.

And the Lord answered me, and said, Write the vision, and make it plain upon tables, that he may run that readeth it. For the vision is yet for the appointed time, and it hasteth toward the end, and shall not lie: though it tarry, wait for it; because it will surely come, it will not delay.

Behold, his soul is puffed up, it is not upright in him: but the just shall live by his faith.[1]

O Lord, thou God to whom vengeance belongeth,
Thou God to whom vengeance belongeth, shine forth.
Lift up thyself, thou judge of the earth:
Render to the proud their desert.
   Lord, how long shall the wicked,
How long shall the wicked triumph?
They prate, they speak arrogantly:
All the workers of iniquity boast themselves.
They break in pieces thy people, O Lord,
And afflict thine heritage.
They slay the widow and the stranger,
And murder the fatherless.
And they say, The Lord shall not see,
Neither shall the God of Jacob consider.
   Consider, ye brutish among the people:
And ye fools, when will ye be wise?
He that planted the ear, shall he not hear?
He that formed the eye, shall he not see?[2]

[1] Hab. 1: 11–2: 4.   [2] Ps. 94: 1–9.

For my thoughts are not your thoughts, neither are your ways my ways, saith the Lord.

For as the heavens are higher than the earth, so are my ways higher than your ways, and my thoughts than your thoughts. For as the rain cometh down and the snow from heaven, and returneth not thither, but watereth the earth, and maketh it bring forth and bud, and giveth seed to the sower and bread to the eater; so shall my word be that goeth forth out of my mouth: it shall not return unto me void, but it shall accomplish that which I please, and it shall prosper in the thing whereto I sent it.[1]

Who is wise, and he shall understand these things; prudent, and he shall know them; for the ways of the Lord are right, and the just shall walk in them; but transgressors shall fall therein.[2]

---

[1] Isa. 55: 8-11.   [2] Hos. 14: 9.

TWELVE

A REMNANT SHALL RETURN[1]

> I will go down with thee into Egypt; and I will also surely bring thee up again.[2]

The doctrine of the Remnant is the last attempt to make sense of the world we know. It follows from the doctrines of choice (Section 10) and of desert (Section 11); for the survival of a Remnant underlines the fact of the destruction of the rest and the reason for it. It also introduces the subject of the next Section, the vision of the future by which alone the present is sustained.

Thus saith the LORD, As the new wine is found in the cluster, and one saith, Destroy it not, for a blessing is in it: so will I do for my servants' sakes, that I may not destroy them all.[3]

As a terebinth, and as an oak, whose stock remaineth, when they are felled.[4]

As the shaking of an olive tree, two or three berries in the top of the uppermost bough.[5]

The remnant of Israel shall not do iniquity, nor speak lies; neither shall a deceitful tongue be found in their mouth.[6]

---

[1] Isa. 10: 21.
[2] Gen. 46: 4.
[3] Isa. 65: 8.
[4] Isa. 6: 13.
[5] Isa. 17: 6.
[6] Zeph. 3: 13.

And it shall come to pass, when all these things are come upon thee, the blessing and the curse, which I have set before thee, and thou shalt call them to mind among all the nations, whither the Lord thy God hath driven thee, and shalt return unto the Lord thy God, and shalt obey his voice according to all that I command thee this day, thou and thy children, with all thine heart, and with all thy soul; that then the Lord thy God will turn thy captivity, and have compassion upon thee, and will return and gather thee from all the peoples, whither the Lord thy God hath scattered thee.

If any of thine outcasts be in the uttermost parts of heaven, from thence will the Lord thy God gather thee, and from thence will he fetch thee.[1]

And it shall come to pass in that day, that the Lord shall set his hand again the second time to recover the remnant of his people, which shall remain, from Assyria, and from Egypt, and from Pathros, and from Cush, and from Elam, and from Shinar, and from Hamath, and from the islands of the sea. And he shall set up an ensign for the nations, and shall assemble the outcasts of Israel, and gather together the dispersed of Judah from the four corners of the earth.[2]

I the Lord change not; therefore ye, O sons of Jacob, are not consumed.[3]

Now it came to pass in the month Chislev, in the twentieth year, as I was in Shushan the palace, that Hanani, one of my brethren, came, he and certain men out of Judah; and I asked them concerning the Jews that had escaped, which were left of the captivity,

[1]Deut. 30: 1–4.   [2]Isa. 11: 11–12.   [3]Mal. 3: 6.

and concerning Jerusalem. And they said unto me, The remnant that are left of the captivity there in the province are in great affliction and reproach: the wall of Jerusalem also is broken down, and the gates thereof are burned with fire.

And it came to pass, when I heard these words, that I sat down and wept, and mourned certain days; and I fasted and prayed before the God of heaven, and said, I beseech thee, O Lord, the God of heaven, the great and terrible God, that keepeth covenant and mercy with them that love him and keep his commandments: let thine ear now be attentive, and thine eyes open, that thou mayest hearken unto the prayer of thy servant, which I pray before thee at this time, day and night, for the children of Israel thy servants, while I confess the sins of the children of Israel, which we have sinned against thee: yea, I and my father's house have sinned. We have dealt very corruptly against thee, and have not kept the commandments, nor the statutes, nor the judgements, which thou commandest thy servant Moses.

Remember, I beseech thee, the word that thou commandest thy servant Moses, saying, If ye trespass, I will scatter you abroad among the peoples: but if ye return to me, and keep my commandments and do them, though your outcasts were in the uttermost part of the heaven, yet will I gather them from thence, and will bring them unto the place that I have chosen to cause my name to dwell there. Now these are thy servants and thy people, whom thou hast redeemed by thy great power, and by thy strong hand.

O Lord, I beseech thee, let now thine ear be attentive to the prayer of thy servant, and to the prayer of thy servants, who delight to fear thy name.[1]

[1] Neh. 1: 1-11.

Unto you that fear my name shall the sun of righteousness arise with healing in his wings.[1]

Thus saith the Lord, The people which were left of the sword found grace in the wilderness; even Israel, when I went to cause him to rest. The Lord appeared of old unto me, saying, Yea, I have loved thee with an everlasting love: therefore with lovingkindness have I drawn thee.

Again will I build thee, and thou shalt be built, O virgin of Israel: again shalt thou be adorned with thy tabrets, and shalt go forth in the dances of them that make merry. Again shalt thou plant vineyards upon the mountains of Samaria: the planters shall plant, and shall enjoy the fruit thereof. For there shall be a day, that the watchman upon the hills of Ephraim shall cry, Arise ye, and let us go up to Zion unto the Lord our God.

For thus saith the Lord, Sing with gladness for Jacob, and shout for the chief of the nations: publish ye, praise ye, and say, O Lord, save thy people, the remnant of Israel. Behold, I will bring them from the north country, and gather them from the uttermost parts of the earth, and with them the blind and the lame, the woman with child and her that travaileth with child together: a great company shall they return hither. They shall come with weeping, and with supplications will I lead them: I will cause them to walk by rivers of waters, in a straight way wherein they shall not stumble: for I am a father to Israel, and Ephraim is my first-born.

Hear the word of the Lord, O ye nations, and declare it in the isles afar off; and say, He that scattered Israel will gather him, and keep him, as a shepherd doth his flock. For the Lord hath ransomed Jacob, and

---

[1] Mal. 4: 2.

redeemed him from the hand of him that was stronger than he.[1]

How lovely are thy tabernacles,
O Lord of hosts!
  My soul longeth, yea, even fainteth for the courts of the Lord;
My heart and my flesh sing for joy unto the living God.
Yea, the sparrow hath found her an house,
And the swallow a nest for herself, where she may lay her young,
Even thine altars, O Lord of hosts,
My King, and my God.
Blessed are they that dwell in thy house:
They will be still praising thee.   [Selah
  Blessed is the man whose strength is in thee;
In whose heart are the high ways to Zion.
Passing through the valley of Weeping they make it a place of springs;
Yea, the early rain covereth it with blessings.
They go from strength to strength,
Every one of them appeareth before God in Zion.[2]

Then fell I down upon my face, and cried with a loud voice, and said, Ah Lord God! wilt thou make a full end of the remnant of Israel?

And the word of the Lord came unto me, saying, Son of man, thy brethren, even thy brethren, the men of thy kindred, and all the house of Israel, all of them, are they unto whom the inhabitants of Jerusalem have said, Get you far from the Lord; unto us is this land given for a possession:

Therefore say, Thus saith the Lord God: Whereas I have removed them far off among the nations, and

---

[1] Jer. 31: 2-11.   [2] Ps. 84: 1-7 (M).

whereas I have scattered them among the countries, yet will I be to them a sanctuary for a little while in the countries where they are come. Therefore say, Thus saith the Lord God: I will gather you from the peoples, and assemble you out of the countries where ye have been scattered, and I will give you the land of Israel. And they shall come thither, and they shall take away all the detestable things thereof and all the abominations thereof from thence.[1]

The hand of the Lord was upon me, and he carried me out in the spirit of the Lord, and set me down in the midst of the valley; and it was full of bones; and he caused me to pass by them round about: and behold, there were very many in the open valley; and lo, they were very dry.

And he said unto me, Son of man, can these bones live? And I answered, O Lord God, thou knowest.

Again he said unto me, Prophesy over these bones, and say unto them, O ye dry bones, hear the word of the Lord. Thus saith the Lord God unto these bones: Behold, I will cause breath to enter into you, and ye shall live. And I will lay sinews upon you, and will bring up flesh upon you, and cover you with skin, and put breath in you, and ye shall live; and ye shall know that I am the Lord.

So I prophesied as I was commanded: and as I prophesied, there was a noise, and behold an earthquake, and the bones came together, bone to his bone. And I beheld, and lo, there were sinews upon them, and flesh came up, and skin covered them above: but there was no breath in them.

Then said he unto me, Prophesy unto the wind, prophesy, son of man, and say to the wind, Thus saith

[1] Ezek. 11: 13-18.

the Lord God: Come from the four winds, O breath, and breathe upon these slain, that they may live.

So I prophesied as he commanded me, and the breath came into them, and they lived, and stood up upon their feet, an exceeding great army.

Then he said unto me, Son of man, these bones are the whole house of Israel: behold, they say, Our bones are dried up, and our hope is lost; we are clean cut off. Therefore prophesy, and say unto them, Thus saith the Lord God: Behold, I will open your graves, and cause you to come up out of your graves, O my people; and I will bring you into the land of Israel. And ye shall know that I am the Lord, when I have opened your graves, and caused you to come up out of your graves, O my people. And I will put my spirit in you, and ye shall live, and I will place you in your own land.[1]

Not by an army, nor by power, but by my spirit, saith the Lord of hosts.[2]

For by strength shall no man prevail.[3]

Thus saith the Lord: I am returned unto Zion, and will dwell in the midst of Jerusalem: and Jerusalem shall be called The city of truth; and the mountains of the Lord of hosts The holy mountain.

Thus saith the Lord of hosts: There shall yet old men and women dwell in the streets of Jerusalem, every man with his staff in his hand for very age. And the streets of the city shall be full of boys and girls playing in the streets thereof.

Thus saith the Lord of hosts: If it be marvellous in the eyes of the remnant of this people in those days,

[1] Ezek. 37: 1–14.   [2] Zech. 4: 6 (m).   [3] 1 Sam. 2: 9.

should it also be marvellous in mine eyes? saith the Lord of hosts.

Thus saith the Lord of hosts: Behold, I will save my people from the east country, and from the west country: and I will bring them, and they shall dwell in the midst of Jerusalem; and they shall be my people, and I will be their God, in truth and in righteousness.[1]

When the Lord turned again the captivity of Zion,
We were like unto them that dream.
Then was our mouth filled with laughter,
And our tongue with singing:
Then said they among the nations,
The Lord hath done great things for them.
The Lord hath done great things for us;
Whereof we are glad.
   Turn again our captivity, O Lord,
As the streams in the South.
They that sow in tears shall reap in joy.
Though he goeth on his way weeping, bearing forth the seed;
He shall come again with joy, bringing his sheaves with him.[2]

Lord, thou hast been favourable unto thy land:
Thou hast brought back the captivity of Jacob.
Thou hast forgiven the iniquity of thy people,
Thou hast covered all their sin.   [Selah
Thou hast taken away all thy wrath:
Thou hast turned thyself from the fierceness of thine anger.
   Turn us, O God of our salvation,
And cause thine indignation toward us to cease.
Wilt thou be angry with us for ever?

[1] Zech. 8: 3-8.   [2] Ps. 126.

Wilt thou draw out thine anger to all generations?
Wilt thou not quicken us again:
That thy people may rejoice in thee?
   Shew us thy mercy, O Lord,
And grant us thy salvation.
I will hear what God the Lord will speak:
For he will speak peace unto his people, and to his
    saints:
But let them turn not again to folly.
Surely his salvation is nigh them that fear him;
That glory may dwell in our land.
   Mercy and truth are met together;
Righteousness and peace have kissed each other.
Truth springeth out of the earth;
And righteousness hath looked down from heaven.
Yea, the Lord shall give that which is good;
And our land shall yield her increase.
Righteousness shall go before him;
And shall make his footsteps a way to walk in.[1]

Then the eyes of the blind shall be opened, and the ears of the deaf shall be unstopped. Then shall the lame man leap as an hart, and the tongue of the dumb shall sing: for in the wilderness shall waters break out, and streams in the desert. And the glowing sand shall become a pool, and the thirsty ground springs of water: in the habitation of jackals, where they lay, shall be grass with reeds and rushes.

And an high way shall be there, and a way and it shall be called The way of holiness.[2]

For I will pour water upon him that is thirsty, and streams upon the dry ground: I will pour my spirit upon thy seed, and my blessing upon thine offspring:

[1] Ps. 85.   [2] Isa. 35: 5–8.

and they shall spring up among the grass, as willows by the watercourses. One shall say, I am the Lord's; and another shall call himself by the name of Jacob; and another shall subscribe with his hand unto the Lord, and surname himself by the name of Israel.[1]

And they shall call them The holy people, The redeemed of the Lord.[2]

And all thy children shall be taught of the Lord; and great shall be the peace of thy children. In righteousness shalt thou be established.[3]

Behold, the days come, saith the Lord, that I will make a new covenant with the house of Israel, and with the house of Judah: not according to the covenant that I made with their fathers in the day that I took them by the hand to bring them out of the land of Egypt; which my covenant they brake, although I was an husband unto them, saith the Lord.

But this is the covenant that I will make with the house of Israel after those days, saith the Lord; I will put my law in their inward parts, and in their heart will I write it; and I will be their God, and they shall be my people: and they shall teach no more every man his neighbour, and every man his brother, saying, Know the Lord: for they shall all know me, from the least of them unto the greatest of them, saith the Lord.[4]

For I will take you from among the nations, and gather you out of all the countries, and will bring you into your own land. And I will sprinkle clean water upon you, and ye shall be clean: from all your filthiness, and from all your idols, will I cleanse you.

[1]Isa. 44: 3-5. [2]Isa. 62: 12. [3]Isa. 54: 13. [4]Jer. 31: 31-34.

A new heart also will I give you, and a new spirit will I put within you: and I will take away the stony heart out of your flesh, and I will give you an heart of flesh. And I will put my spirit within you.[1]

And I will give them one heart, and I will put a new spirit within you; and I will take the stony heart out of their flesh, and will give them an heart of flesh: that they may walk in my statutes, and keep mine ordinances, and do them: and they shall be my people, and I will be their God.

But as for them whose heart walketh after the heart of their detestable things and their abominations, I will bring their way upon their own heads, saith the Lord God.[2]

[1]Ezek. 36: 24–27.   [2]Ezek. 11: 19–21.

THIRTEEN

THE VISION FOR THE APPOINTED TIME[1]

> Son of man, what is this proverb that ye have
> in the land of Israel, saying, The days are
> prolonged, and every vision faileth?[2]

'*Where there is no vision the people cast off restraint*' (*Prov. 29: 18*) *or, as the Authorised Version has it, with more sense but less philological justification, the 'people perisheth'. Utopias have always cajoled, and eased the burdens of, mankind. The notable point about the Utopias of the Hebrew Scriptures is that the future they depict is in principle open to all. Even when, as so often, the central place in the picture is occupied by the restored Israel, it is an Israel which has been thrice purged and to which 'all flesh' has been added. In 'that day', indeed, it is rather 'all flesh' which includes Israel than Israel which includes 'all flesh'. The typical prophetic message is addressed to all humankind: 'He hath shewed thee,* O *man, what is good.*'

The voice of one that crieth, Prepare ye in the wilderness the way of the Lord, make straight in the desert a high way for our God.

Every valley shall be exalted, and every mountain and hill shall be made low: and the crooked shall be made straight, and the rough places plain.

And the glory of the Lord shall be revealed, and all flesh shall see it together.[3]

And it shall come to pass afterward, that I will pour out my spirit upon all flesh; and your sons and your

[1]Hab. 2: 3.   [2]Ezek. 12: 22.   [3]Isa. 40: 3–5.

daughters shall prophesy, your old men shall dream dreams, your young men shall see visions: and also upon the servants and upon the handmaids in those days will I pour out my spirit.[1]

There shall be poured upon us a spirit from on high.[2]

And your eyes shall see and ye shall say, The Lord be magnified beyond the border of Israel.[3]

Look unto me, and be ye saved, all the ends of the earth: for I am God, and there is none else.[4]

The Lord God which gathereth the outcasts of Israel saith, Yet will I gather others to him, beside his own that are gathered.[5]

The stranger, that is not of thy people Israel, shall come out of a far country for thy name's sake.[6]

For the earth shall be filled with the knowledge of the glory of the Lord, as the waters cover the sea.[7]

And it shall come to pass in the latter days, that the mountain of the Lord's house shall be established in the top of the mountains, and it shall be exalted above the hills; and peoples shall flow unto it. And many nations shall go and say, Come ye, and let us go up to the mountain of the Lord, and to the house of the God of Jacob; and he will teach us of his ways, and we will walk in his paths: for out of Zion shall go forth the law, and the word of the Lord from Jerusalem.

And he shall judge between many peoples, and shall

---

[1] Joel, 2: 28–29. [2] Mal. 1: 5. [4] Isa. 56: 8. [7] Hab. 2: 14.
[2] Isa. 32: 15 (OA). [3] Isa. 45: 22. [6] 1 Kings 8: 41.

reprove strong nations afar off; and they shall beat their swords into plowshares, and their spears into pruning-hooks: nation shall not lift up sword against nation, neither shall they learn war any more. But they shall sit every man under his vine and under his fig tree; and none shall make them afraid: for the mouth of the Lord of hosts hath spoken it.[1]

For all the armour of the armed man in the tumult, and the garments rolled in blood, shall even be for burning, for fuel of fire.[2]

He maketh wars to cease unto the end of the earth;
He breaketh the bow, and cutteth the spear in sunder;
He burneth the chariots in the fire.[3]

The extortioner is brought to nought, spoiling ceaseth, the oppressors are consumed out of the land.[4]

And he will destroy in this mountain the face of the covering that is cast over all peoples, and the veil that is spread over all nations. He hath swallowed up death for ever; and the Lord God will wipe away tears from off all faces; and the reproach of his people shall he take away from off all the earth: for the Lord hath spoken it.[5]

I will ransom them from the power of the grave; I will redeem them from death: O death, where are thy plagues? O grave, where is thy destruction?[6]

Thy dead shall live; my dead bodies shall arise. Awake and sing, ye that dwell in the dust: for thy dew is as

[1] Mic. 4: 1-4 (OA).
[2] Isa. 9: 5.
[3] Ps. 46: 9.
[4] Isa. 16: 4.
[5] Isa. 25: 7-8.
[6] Hos. 13: 14.

the dew of herbs, and the earth shall cast forth the dead.[1]

And there shall come forth a shoot out of the stock of Jesse, and a branch out of his roots shall bear fruit: and the spirit of the Lord shall rest upon him, the spirit of wisdom and understanding, the spirit of counsel and might, the spirit of knowledge and of the fear of the Lord; and his delight shall be in the fear of the Lord: and he shall not judge after the sight of his eyes, neither reprove after the hearing of his ears: but with righteousness shall he judge the poor, and reprove with equity for the meek of the earth: and he shall smite the earth with the rod of his mouth, and with the breath of his lips shall he slay the wicked. And righteousness shall be the girdle of his loins, and faithfulness the girdle of his reins.

And the wolf shall dwell with the lamb, and the leopard shall lie down with the kid; and the calf and the young lion and the fatling together; and a little child shall lead them. And the cow and the bear shall feed; their young ones shall lie down together: and the lion shall eat straw like the ox. And the sucking child shall play on the hole of the asp, and the weaned child shall put his hand on the basilisk's den.

They shall not hurt nor destroy in all my holy mountain: for the earth shall be full of the knowledge of the Lord, as the waters cover the sea.[2]

For then will I turn to the peoples a pure language, that they may all call upon the name of the Lord, to serve him with one consent.[3]

Unto me every knee shall bend and every tongue shall swear.[4]

[1] Isa. 26: 19. [2] Isa. 11. 1–9. [3] Zeph. 3: 9. [4] Isa. 45: 23.

Behold, the days come, saith the Lord God, that I will send a famine in the land, not a famine of bread, nor a thirst for water, but of hearing the words of the Lord.[1]

Ho, every one that thirsteth, come ye to the waters, and he that hath no money; come ye, buy, and eat; yea, come, buy wine and milk without money and without price.
  Wherefore do ye spend money for that which is not bread? and your labour for that which satisfieth not? hearken diligently unto me, and eat ye that which is good, and let your soul delight itself in fatness.[2]

O taste and see that the Lord is good:
Blessed is the man that trusteth in him.[3]

O thou that hearest prayer,
Unto thee shall all flesh come.[4]

All nations whom thou hast made shall come and worship before thee, O Lord.[5]

For mine house shall be called an house of prayer for all peoples.[6]

Thus saith the Lord of hosts: It shall yet come to pass, that there shall come peoples, and the inhabitants of many cities: and the inhabitants of one city shall go to another, saying, Let us go speedily to intreat the favour of the Lord, and to seek the Lord of hosts: I will go also. Yea, many peoples and strong nations shall come to seek the Lord of hosts in Jerusalem, and to intreat the favour of the Lord.

[1] Amos 5: 11.
[2] Isa. 55: 1–2.
[3] Ps. 34: 8.
[4] Ps. 65: 2.
[5] Ps. 86: 9.
[6] Isa. 56: 7.

Thus saith the Lord of hosts: In those days it shall come to pass, that ten men shall take hold, out of all the languages of the nations, shall even take hold of the skirt of him that is a Jew, saying, We will go with you, for we have heard that God is with you.[1]

Glorious things are spoken of thee,
O city of God. [Selah
I will make mention of Rahab and Babylon as among them that know me.
Behold Philistia, and Tyre, with Ethiopia;
This one was born there.
Yea, of Zion it shall be said, This one and that one was born in her;
And the Most High himself shall establish her.
The Lord shall count, when he writeth up the peoples,
This one was born there.[2] [Selah

And it shall come to pass in that day, that the root of Jesse, which standeth for an ensign of the peoples, unto him shall the nations seek; and his resting place shall be glorious.[3]

And many nations shall join themselves to the Lord in that day, and shall be my people.[4]

In that day there shall be five cities in the land of Egypt that speak the language of Canaan, and swear to the Lord of hosts; one shall be called The city of destruction.

In that day shall there be an altar to the Lord in the midst of the land of Egypt, and a pillar at the border thereof to the Lord. And it shall be for a sign and for a witness unto the Lord of hosts in the land of

[1]Zech. 8: 20-23.   [2]Ps. 87: 3-6.   [3]Isa. 11: 10.   [4]Zech. 2: 11.

Egypt: for they shall cry unto the Lord because of the oppressors, and he shall send them a saviour, and a defender, and he shall deliver them. And the Lord shall be known to Egypt, and the Egyptians shall know the Lord in that day; yea, they shall worship with sacrifice and oblation, and shall vow a vow unto the Lord, and shall perform it. And the Lord shall smite Egypt, smiting and healing; and they shall return unto the Lord and he shall be intreated of them, and shall heal them.

In that day shall there be a high way out of Egypt to Assyria, and the Assyrian shall come into Egypt, and the Egyptian into Assyria; and the Egyptians shall worship with the Assyrians.

In that day shall Israel be the third with Egypt and with Assyria, a blessing in the midst of the earth: for that the Lord of hosts hath blessed them, saying, Blessed be Egypt my people, and Assyria the work of my hands, and Israel mine inheritance.[1]

And it shall be said in that day, Lo, this is our God; we have waited for him, and he will save us: this is the Lord; we have waited for him, we will be glad and rejoice in his salvation.[2]

In that day shall a man look unto his Maker, and his eyes shall have respect to the Holy One of Israel.[3]

In that day shall the Lord be one, and his name one.[4]

The God of the whole earth shall he be called.[5]

[1] Isa. 19: 18–24.
[2] Isa. 25: 9.
[3] Isa. 17: 7.
[4] Zech. 14: 9.
[5] Isa. 54: 5.

FOURTEEN

THE END OF THE MATTER[1]

> Peace, peace, to him that is far off and to him that is near, saith the Lord; and I will heal him.[2]

But is there an end to the matter? The Rabbis, quoting Ps. 84: 7, speak of an eternal quest. The seekers for wisdom, they say, have no rest either in this world or in the next, for they go continuously 'from strength to strength'.

Oh that I knew where I might find him,
That I might come even to his seat![3]

*

He hath shewed thee, O man, what is good; and what doth the Lord require of thee, but to do justly, and to love mercy, and to walk humbly with thy God.[4]

*

The Lord our God be with us, as he was with our fathers: let him not leave us, nor forsake us: that he may incline our hearts unto him, to walk in all his ways, and to keep his commandments, and his statutes, and his judgements, which he commanded our fathers.[5]

*

The eternal God is thy dwelling place,
And underneath are the everlasting arms.[6]

[1] Eccles. 12: 13. [3] Job. 23: 3. [5] 1 Kings 8: 57–58.
[2] Isa. 57: 19.   [4] Mic. 6: 8.   [6] Deut. 32: 27.

THE END

For Product Safety Concerns and Information please contact our EU representative GPSR@taylorandfrancis.com
Taylor & Francis Verlag GmbH, Kaufingerstraße 24, 80331 München, Germany

www.ingramcontent.com/pod-product-compliance
Lightning Source LLC
Chambersburg PA
CBHW061839300426
44115CB00013B/2451